THE
ARMOR
OF
LOVE

THE
ARMOR
OF
LOVE

ELAINE BOONE

WinePressPublishing
Great Books, Defined.

WinePress Publishing is honored to present this title in partnership with the author. The views expressed or implied in this work are those of the author. WinePress provides our imprint seal representing design excellence, creative content and high quality production. To learn more about Responsible Publishing™ visit www.winepresspublishing.com.

Unless otherwise indicated, Scripture is taken from *Thinline Bible, New International Version*® Copyright © 1996 by Zondervan Corporation.

Unless otherwise indicated, Scripture is taken from the *Holy Bible, New International Version*®, *NIV*®. Copyright © 1973, 1978, 1984 by Biblica, Inc.™ Used by permission of Zondervan. All rights reserved worldwide. WWW.ZONDERVAN.COM

References to the *King James Bible* are taken from: *KJV Reference Bible*, Grand Rapids, MI: Zondervan Publishing House, Copyright© 1994.

References to the *New King James Bible* are taken from: *New Geneva Study Bible*, Nashville: Thomas Nelson Publishers, Copyright © 1979, 1980, 1982, 1995.

References to *The Bible Encyclopaedia* are taken from: *The International Standard Bible Encyclopaedia*, Orr, James, general editor, John L. Nuelsen, and Edgar Y. Mullins assistant editors, Grand Rapids, MI: Wm. B. Eerdmans Publishing Co., Copyright © 1939: Five Volumes.

References to *Vine's Greek Dictionary* are taken from: *Vine, W. E. Expository Dictionary of Old and New Testament Words*. Old Testament edited by F. F. Bruce. New Jersey: Fleming H. Revell Company, Copyright © 1981.

References to Webster are taken from: *Webster's New World Dictionary of American English*, Neufeldt, Victoria, Editor in Chief, David B. Guralnik, editor in chief Emeritus 3rd college edition, New York: Simon & Schuster, Inc., 1991, 1988, 1994.

References to *The Bible Dictionary* are taken from: *The New Compact Bible Dictionary*, Grand Rapids, MI: Zondervan Publishing House, 1967.

References to Strong's is taken from: *The Exhaustive Concordance of The Bible,* Strong, James, Peabody, MA: Hendrickson Publishers.

References to *The Interlinear Bible* are taken from: *Interlinear Greek-English New Testament*, Berry, George Ricker, Grand Rapids, MI: Baker Books, 1897, 1999.

Scripture references marked NASB are taken from the *New American Standard Bible,* Nashville, TN: Holman Bible Publishers, Copyright © 1960, 1962, 1963, 1968, 1971, 1972, 1973, 1975, 1977 by The Lockman Foundation. Used by permission.

ISBN 13: 978-1-4141-1436-1
ISBN 10: 1-4141-1436-2
Library of Congress Catalog Card Number: 2009903163

Dedicated to my daughter Laurie,

Who is devoted to her LORD and Savior, Jesus Christ,

Practices Christ's unfailing love,

Has "learned the secret of being content" (Phil. 4:12),

Makes "every effort to live in peace with all men

And to be holy" (Heb. 12:14).

She doesn't waver or wear a mask in her Christian walk,

But aims for perfection

By keeping "in step with the Spirit" (Gal. 5:25).

CONTENTS

ACKNOWLEDGMENTS

FIRST AND FOREMOST, I thank my heavenly Father, who graciously loves and forgives me through the shed blood of my Savior, Jesus Christ, who imputed his righteousness to me. I thank the Holy Spirit, who counsels and guides me with the truths of Scripture and who patiently instructed me throughout the writing of this book. Thank you LORD that your unfailing love surrounds us when we trust in you (Ps. 32:10).

I wish to thank my children: Dave, Virginia, Gene, Heidi, Doug, Laurie, Brian, Judy, my eighteen grandchildren and even my five great-grandchildren for their love, prayers, and encouragement, because they knew that writing this book was an overwhelming task. I love all of you very much and thank the LORD, daily, that he has given each one of you to me as treasured gifts.

I thank my sisters: Arlene, who read the first draft and continually prayed for me; and Marilyn, who was so excited about the book but was never able to see or read it because she went to be with the LORD on July 1, 2005. Thanks, Vern, for your extra help and encouragement. I thank my deceased parents, who encouraged church attendance, regular Bible reading, and provided me the opportunity of attending Christian schools.

I thank numerous friends, former co-workers, and my church family for their many years of prayer and encouragement. I especially thank Betty, Dee, Sally, Helen, Beth, Karl, and Pastor Al, with added thanks to Harriet for her extra, kind, unselfish help.

Finally, I wish to thank all those at Winepress Publishing: Lee, my editor, Tammy, my project manager, Mike, Athena, my cover designer, Abigail, my publicity advisor, Kevin, my website designer, and everyone else who contributed to the publishing of this book. With their faithful commitment, this message of love from our LORD will reach way beyond my life and immediate family.

PREFACE

RATHER THAN PUT the words "emphasis mine," I have taken the liberty to italicize words or phrases for the sake of emphasis. I am hoping these words and phrases will impact you as much as they have me. I also put a few questions after each chapter in case you would like to use this book as a devotional or group study.

The Armor of Love, from beginning to end, is about our reliance on the power of the Holy Spirit—mentally, emotionally, physically, and spiritually. As Jesus points out to Nicodemus, a Jewish leader, in John 3:3, 8, we must be "born again," "born of the Spirit," or we will not see the kingdom of God. On the day of Pentecost, Peter preached this same message: "Repent and be baptized, every one of you, in the name of Jesus Christ for the forgiveness of your sins. And you will receive the gift of the Holy Spirit" (Acts 2:38).

True love is found only in God, through belief in Jesus Christ, as our Savior and Master, along with a willingness to pursue his character of humbleness and gentleness. Christ's humbleness of love is recorded for us in Phil. 2:1–11. He was willing to leave his "equality with God" in heaven, and become nothing for us. Christ "humbled himself and became obedient to death—even death on the cross." When we fully surrender our selfish, conceited hearts (see Phil. 2:1–4) to Christ, our character will be transformed (see Rom. 12:2) to one of love, humbleness and gentleness (fruit of the Holy Spirit).

We must *all* make every effort to know, understand, and experience what it means to fully surrender our heart to a "born again" experience (see 2 Peter 1:10, 11). God's living, active word (Heb. 4:12) guides us in this surrender, through the power of the Holy Spirit, and gives us the gift of faith to believe and receive Christ as our Savior. For "without [sure and certain] faith it is impossible to please God" (Heb. 11:1, 6).

> If you have any encouragement from being united with Christ, if any comfort from his love, if any fellowship with the Spirit, if any tenderness and compassion, then make my joy complete by being like-minded, having the same love, being one in spirit and purpose.... Your attitude should be the same as that of Christ Jesus.
>
> (Phil 2:1–5)

> "A new command I give you: Love one another. As I have loved you, so you must love one another. By this all men will know that you are my disciples, if you love one another."
>
> (John 13:34–35)

> Whatever is true, whatever is noble, whatever is right, whatever is pure, whatever is lovely, whatever is admirable—if anything is excellent or praiseworthy—think about such things.
>
> (Phil. 4:8)

> As God's chosen people, holy and dearly loved, clothe yourselves with compassion, kindness, humility, gentleness and patience. Bear with each other and forgive whatever grievances you may have against one another. Forgive as the Lord forgave you. And over all these virtues put on love, which binds them all together in perfect unity.
>
> (Col. 3:12–14)

> The fruit of the Spirit is love, joy, peace, patience, kindness, goodness, faithfulness, gentleness and self-control.
>
> (Gal. 5:22–23)

INTRODUCTION

ONE MORNING ABOUT 30 years ago, as I struggled with painful emotional problems, marriage conflicts, and insecurities, I heard the LORD say to me, "You need to learn how to love." Since childhood, my heart and mind lacked the loving confidence they needed to overcome their hollow and empty nature. I was ignorant in my knowledge of love as God intended it to be. My thinking about love or its practice up to that time was learned and based on a comparison to other Christians and their ignorance of love. They weren't well versed about biblical love either. I was adapting behavior and practicing views based on lies.

I believe I also failed to grasp biblical love because it seems that, as I read Scripture, I was never "born of the Spirit" (John 3:8). Once the Spirit enters, our desires become like the new believers at Pentecost. "They devoted themselves to the apostles teaching, and to the fellowship, to the breaking of bread and to prayer" (Acts 2:42). And our desires change from earthly wisdom to heavenly wisdom: purity, love with peace, consideration, submission, mercy and good fruit, impartiality and sincerity (see James 3:13–17).

Soon after I heard God telling me that I needed to learn how to love, I shared this with a friend and she suggested that I start practicing the steps of faith found in 2 Peter 1:3–11. In summary,

these steps include: goodness, knowledge, self-control, perseverance, godliness, brotherly kindness, and love—one builds upon
the other. "If you possess these qualities in increasing measure,
they will keep you from being ineffective and unproductive in your
knowledge of our LORD Jesus Christ" (verse 8). These precious
promises keep us in Christ's divine nature so we can escape the
corruptions in the world caused by evil desires.

As time went on, the time I spent in the Bible became a priority
and a necessity because, like Job (42:5), I had only heard about
God. I needed to see and experience him. I needed the wisdom of
Proverbs 2. I needed to accept his words; store up his commands;
turn my ear toward wisdom; apply my heart to understanding; call
out for insight; cry aloud for understanding; look for it as for silver;
and search for it as hidden treasure. Only then would I understand
the fear of the LORD and be able to walk in his ways.

According to David Henderson, the Bible is, "a single fabric
of thought stretching from front to back...and is about God's
unstoppable passion to be known, loved, and served—through
Jesus Christ—by those he has made."[1]

Scripture began to make a tremendous impact in my life, yet
my marriage problems weren't improving. The more I sought the
LORD, the more it seemed my husband distanced himself from me.
I vacillated between God and my husband because I didn't want to
choose between them, but, truth be told, my husband's love was
already cold. As time went on, I began to realize that only the love
of the LORD and his Word could give me the strength to face the
days, months, and years ahead. My husband and I separated and
two years later, we divorced.

The Holy Spirit began teaching me the difference between head
and heart knowledge and I saw the similarity to Dr. Ed Murphy's
point regarding "the traditional Western logical-analytical approach
towards evangelism."[2] Heart knowledge derives its power from
the Holy Spirit and that power confronts our sinfulness, leads us
to true repentance, and Christ's forgiveness. Head knowledge is
intellectual in nature, while heart knowledge is a deep desire to
learn and grow in God's Word and to obey him in all things. In my

experience, head knowledge gave me plenty of information about Jesus and the consequences of not believing in him, but that didn't unleash the power of the Holy Spirit in my life and it didn't lead to sincere repentance.

So many major life events occurred after my divorce. Twice, I had to move and downsize my style of living. I took correspondence courses from Liberty University in Virginia—studying theology (which included a trip to Israel for extra credits), psychology, and counseling. I worked in retail for thirteen years and then for a Christian non-profit organization that gave me the opportunity to spend a week observing their work in Mali, Africa. After eight years, I retired. I experienced the graciousness of the LORD and his answer to many prayers when he miraculously healed me from brain surgery and kept me from prison after a fatal car accident.

Then, an amazing thing happened. As I was praying for direction, God spoke to me again and told me to write a book. From a former message about Romans 8:28, the pastor emphasized that we could *know* that everything God allows into our lives works for the good of those who love him. However, writing a book caught me totally off guard. Writing (except for college research papers) and keeping a journal is something I've always shied away from because it's difficult for me to put my thoughts into words. My response to God was, "But that's impossible, I don't know how to write." God reminded me how he dealt with Moses when he objected to God's direction, and this reminder drew me back from the impossible. I simply needed to trust and obey.

Over the next few days God did just that—the Holy Spirit gave me the content, title, and message. I had also prayed for added assurance when I shared his message and my subject with my sister and a couple of friends. They never hesitated in their support, but affirmed me immediately and also offered to pray for me while I worked. They were even somewhat surprised that I questioned my ability. Oswald Chambers, one of the spiritual giants in my life, gave me more assurance:

Suddenly Jesus appears to us, the fires are kindled,...then we have to learn to keep the secret of the burning heart that will go through anything.... If it be an emotion kindled by the Spirit of God and you do not let that emotion have its right issue in your life, it will react on a lower level.... We cannot stay on the mount of transfiguration, but we must obey the light we received there; we must act it out. When God gives a vision, transact business on that line, no matter what it costs.[3]

You'll find that I've organized this book using 1 Corinthians 13—the "love chapter." For reference, here are the specific verses:

If I speak in the tongues of men and of angels, but have not love, I am only a resounding gong or a clanging cymbal. If I have the gift of prophecy and can fathom all mysteries and all knowledge, and if I have a faith that can move mountains, but have not love, I am nothing. If I give all I possess to the poor and surrender my body to the flames, but have not love, I gain nothing. Love is patient, love is kind. It does not envy, it does not boast, it is not proud. It is not rude, it is not self-seeking, it is not easily angered, it keeps no record of wrongs. Love does not delight in evil but rejoices with the truth. It always protects, always trusts, always hopes, always perseveres. Love never fails.

(1 Cor. 13:1–8)

While writing about the concept of love, I realized something— our tendency to label God's love as unconditional. Yet, the Bible never uses that term; instead, it uses terms like, "a covenant of love," "enduring," "unfailing," "everlasting," and "abounding love." The assurance we find in God's unfailing, enduring boundaries of love and forgiveness never wavers, even when we choose to disobey and disregard the work of the Holy Spirit. He remains faithful, compassionate, and trustworthy, always seeking to win us back to him. It is my prayer that as you read this book you will receive the same blessing God has given me as I experienced and learned how to love. And I pray that you discover the depths of his enduring love.

CHAPTER 1

THE HOLY SPIRIT

IN 1 CORINTHIANS, Paul quotes Isaiah 64:4 as saying, "It is written"—noting the importance of the written Word of God. He wanted the Corinthian church to know that God loves his chosen people just as much in the New Testament era as he did in the Old Testament era. "'No eye has seen, no ear has heard, no mind has conceived what God has prepared for those who love him'—but God has revealed it to us by his Spirit" (1 Cor. 2:9–10).

I believe our Christian culture has been remiss in our practice, ideas, and understanding of love. Since "God is love" and we only learn how to love through the power of the Holy Spirit, then a proper knowledge of that love only comes as we search the Scriptures and then rely upon the Holy Spirit. For the Spirit of God searches the deep things of God (see 1 Cor. 2:10). Too often, we neglect the discussion and practice of the fruit of the Holy Spirit. We "grieve" the Holy Spirit (Eph. 4:30) when we neglect him, becoming weak in many spiritual areas: our strength, our submission, love, faith, joy, hope, trust, study of the Bible, and the ability to "have the mind of Christ" (1 Cor. 2:16).

Often, the Holy Spirit is equated more with the Pentecostal movement—speaking in tongues, etc.—than with the rest of Protestantism, and the result is that we suffer a severe loss of the

Spirit's benefits. One of those benefits is the overwhelming sense that God loves us.

The Holy Spirit is the One who keeps God's enduring, unfailing love flowing directly to us, through Christ, every moment of every day. J. I. Packer tells us the Holy Spirit "is a floodlight ministry in relation to Jesus, a matter of spotlighting Jesus' glory before our spiritual eyes and of matchmaking between us and him. He does not call attention to himself or present himself to us for direct fellowship as the Father and the Son do; his role and his joy is to further our fellowship with them both by glorifying the Son as the object for our faith and then witnessing to our adoption through the Son into the Father's family."[1]

THE PERSON OF THE HOLY SPIRIT

Tony Evans prompted my initial search for a greater understanding of the Person of the Holy Spirit when I read his book, *The Promise*. When Jesus said, "It is to your advantage that I go away; for if I do not go away, the Helper will not come to you; but if I depart, I will send Him to you" (John 16:7 NKJV), he was explaining the importance of the Holy Spirit in our lives after he went to heaven. Evans pointed out that, "If Jesus Christ were on earth today in His bodily presence, we would be a defeated, decimated people."[2]

Jesus could only be in one place at a time in his human form, but the Holy Spirit can go everywhere with us. In that position, the testimony of the Holy Spirit about Jesus will provide the peace and comfort we need in this life. "Peace I leave with you; my peace I give you.... Do not let your hearts be troubled and do not be afraid" (John 14:27). The Holy Spirit, the *truth*, lives *with* us and *in* us (see John 14:17).

Evans also noted why many individuals lack knowledge and reliance on the Holy Spirit. We think that we know all about him, but the reality is, we generally know very little about him and we only rely on him when we believe we can't accomplish everything in our own strength (see Gal. 3:3). "The fact is," Evans says, "His role is the indispensable factor in determining whether you

2

win or lose spiritually, whether you are a failure or a success as a
Christian.... If you are going to experience the benefits of the Holy
Spirit's power, He must have more of you. You don't need more of
Him. The key...is obedience."[3]

THE POWER OF THE HOLY SPIRIT

As I continued my study about the Holy Spirit, I discovered the
marvelous and awesome words of Ephesians 1:17–20. We, "who
believe" receive from God the same power of "mighty strength"
that the Holy Spirit used when he raised Jesus from the dead.
That was Paul's prayer for the Corinthian church, "I keep asking
that the God of our Lord Jesus Christ, the glorious Father" would
give them the "Spirit of wisdom and revelation" so that they may
"know him better" and have the eyes of their heart enlightened.
We must have our eyes opened so we may know the Holy Spirit
better and the hope to which he has called us, an inheritance and
power promised to all who believe in Christ.

What an awesome revelation this was to me! By possessing
the Spirit, we have the same power inside of us that raised Christ
from the dead. Not only is that an awesome revelation, it's a gift
the Father has given to us! When we repent, and confess faith in
Christ, we receive the Holy Spirit "without limit" (John 3:34) and
he is "poured out on us generously through Jesus Christ our Savior,
so that, having been justified by his grace, we might become heirs
having the hope of eternal life" (Titus 3:6–7).

From what I have always been taught or understood, it seems
necessary to keep asking for a greater measure of the Holy Spirit,
but I do not believe that is what the Bible teaches. It is like Tony
Evans said, "We don't need more of Him, but He needs more of us!"
Our problem is, we do not draw on, dwell in, trust, appropriate, or
rely on that generosity. God gives us the gift of his Spirit because he
wants us to be "rooted and established" by faith in his boundless
love (Eph. 3:17–18). How sad that we do not fully understand the
place of the Holy Spirit in our lives.

The Holy Spirit is our Counselor. Think about that. How often have you wished you had someone who was readily available to hear your trials, temptations, and sufferings? You already have all of that in the Person of the Holy Spirit. His power, within us, enables our love, our self-discipline, and keeps us filled "to the measure of all the fullness of God" (Eph. 3:19). Failing to recognize the presence of the Holy Spirit creates a heart lacking in praise and thankfulness.

I love what Andrew Murray said about the power of the Spirit:

> There is a difference between the power of the Spirit as a gift and the power of the Spirit for the grace of a holy life. A man may often have a measure of the power of the Spirit, but if there is not a large measure of the Spirit as the Spirit of grace and holiness, the defect will be evident in his work.... But, a man who is separated unto the Holy Spirit is a man who is given up to say: "Father, let the Holy Spirit have full dominion over me, in my home, in my temper, in every word of my tongue, in every thought of my heart, in every feeling toward my fellow-men."[4]

THE WORK OF THE HOLY SPIRIT

When we repent, believe in, and confess Jesus Christ as our Savior and LORD, the Holy Spirit washes us with rebirth, renews us (see Titus 3:5), and seals us (see Eph. 1:13) through baptism (see Matt. 3:11). According to Jesus, The Holy Spirit testifies about him (see John 15:26) and guides us into all the truth that he spoke while here on earth (see John 14:26). He also convicts "the world of guilt in regard to sin and righteousness and judgment: in regard to sin, because men do not believe in me; in regard to righteousness, because I am going to the Father;...and in regard to judgment, because the prince of this world now stands condemned" (John 16:8–11).

After our conviction and rebirth, the Holy Spirit sanctifies us (see 2 Thess. 2:13), keeps us "filled" (see Eph. 5:18), and as the "sword of the Spirit, which is the word of God" protects us from the spiritual forces of evil (Eph. 6:17). Yet, because we are so prone to listen to Satan's lies, we keep wandering away, disobeying the Holy Spirit, and removing ourselves from his unlimited supply of love and grace. How grateful we can be that the Holy Spirit, like God, never leaves us and welcomes us back with joy when we come back in true repentance, so he can further our maturity in Christ.

Before we move on to the Holy Spirit's next work—spiritual gifts, I would like to point out something else I learned during my search about love and the fruit of the Spirit. In Matt. 7:16, 20 and 12:33, Jesus told us that Christians would be recognized by their fruit. When he did so he was referring to the fruit of the Holy Spirit as found in Galatians 5:22–23: "love, joy, peace, patience, kindness, goodness, faithfulness, gentleness and self-control." We are *not* recognized by our works, but by the actual fruit of the Holy Spirit, listed above, which is manifested in us while we do our work and service for Christ. Jesus said, "I am the vine; you are the branches. If a man remains in me and I in him, he will bear much fruit; apart from me you can do nothing" (John 15:5).

MISCONCEPTION OF SPIRITUAL GIFTS

Our knowledge about the Holy Spirit isn't complete unless we address spiritual gifts. Everyone who believes in Christ will have certain gifts manifested and empowered by the Holy Spirit in them. These gifts are listed and explained in Romans 12, Ephesians 4, and 1 Corinthians 12–14. Paul deals with the Corinthian church about this because they placed their spiritual gifts above the practice of love. Spiritual gifts are not given to promote either self or our works. The Holy Spirit manifests himself in us to bring glory and honor to Christ.

Every gift is given to edify the body of Christ, until we reach unity in the faith, gain knowledge of the Son of God and become mature (see Eph. 4:12–13). If the Holy Spirit lives in our heart, he will give gifts to each of us "as he determines" (1 Cor. 12:11), but the gifts of love and prayer are given to *all* of us. Love and prayer maintain our other gifts (see Eph. 6:13, 18). When someone speaks

5

in a tongue, he or she doesn't speak to men but to God. So if one speaks in a tongue, he or she must also interpret; otherwise, that person is only edifying self. Paul called everyone to prophesy instead, so that the church would be edified (see 1 Cor. 14:1–4).

I took my first spiritual gifts test while I was involved with a singles group right after my divorce. A number of churches were using that same test to find the correct talent, passion, or role of each member to plug him or her into the area of the church where he or she was best suited, rather than using whomever was available. This system wasn't inappropriate, but, like the Corinthians, the concentration on spiritual gifts became more important than learning and practicing love. Shortly afterward, I saw a video presentation by R. C. Sproul, Sr., during which he said much the same thing—Christians are "preoccupied with the gifts of the Spirit to the neglect of the fruit of the Spirit.... Gifts apart from love adds up to futility."[5]

During my childhood, we were taught the same thing—that our performance, usually in comparison to others, is the standard by which we are to measure our spiritual life. J. I. Packer said this, "To know God's love is indeed heaven on earth.... One could wish that this aspect of his ministry was prized more highly than it is at the present time. With a perversity as pathetic as it is impoverishing, we have become preoccupied today with the extraordinary, sporadic, non-universal ministries of the Spirit to the neglect of the ordinary, general ones...peace, joy, hope, and love.... Yet the latter is much more important than the former."[6]

This brings me to another important concept. Gordon MacDonald impressed me with his writings about having an orderly cultivated inner garden. To maintain that garden we must not confuse the actual cultivation of our inner mind, emotions, and heart by the Holy Spirit with this performance/works theology, which McDonald says, "Our Western cultural values have helped to blind us to this tendency. We are naively inclined to believe that the most publicly active person is also the most privately spiritual. We assume that the larger the church, the greater its heavenly blessing. The more information about the Bible a person possesses, we think, the closer he must be to God."[7] I was very grateful that the LORD directed me to these well-known Bible-believing scholars who confirmed Paul's teachings to the Corinthians, because their message saved me from falling into error.

Jesus, our model for living the Christian life, never used spiritual gifts as the indicator of our discipleship—he only used love as an indicator. "As I have loved you, so you must love one another. By this all men will know that you are my disciples, if you love one another" (John 13:34–35).

According to Dietrich Bonhoeffer: "Works are done by human hands, fruit thrusts upward and grows all unbeknown to the tree which bears it. Works are dead, fruit is alive, and bears the seed which will bring forth more fruit. Works can subsist on their own, fruit cannot exist apart from the tree. Fruit is always the miraculous, the created; it is never the result of willing, but always a growth."[8] As the Holy Spirit works this growth of his fruit, we receive "life" and a mind of "peace" as He shapes and conforms us into the likeness of God's Son (see Rom. 8:6, 29).

Paul, in the three texts in which he speaks specifically about spiritual gifts, shows that love is the center of everything. In Romans 12, he speaks about transformation of our mind leading to a life of genuine love toward all people apart from any self-centeredness. In Ephesians 4:2, 15–16, he calls for humility, gentleness, and patience wherein the church speaks the truth and builds itself up in love, as each part does its work. In 1 Corinthians 12–14, he places emphasis on "the most excellent way…. Faith, hope and love. But the greatest of these is love…. Love never fails." The armor of love is Christ within us, manifested through spiritual gifts, which then builds and creates unity and maturity.

WALK "BY" THE HOLY SPIRIT

The Corinthian church had fallen into immaturity, instability, divisions, jealousy and envy, lawsuits, marital difficulties, sexual immorality, and misuse of spiritual gifts because they neglected the pursuit of love. We, today, need to beware of the creeping godlessness coming into the life of the church (see 2 Tim. 3:1–5). We are continually being drawn away from the pursuit of God's scriptural directives, such as "If we *live by* the Spirit, let us also *walk by* the Spirit" (Gal. 5:25 RSV), and, "Be imitators of God, as beloved children. And walk in love, as Christ loved us…" (Eph. 5:1–2 RSV).

Without love, we are unable to honor and glorify Christ. That was the condition of my life until I started this journey. After my divorce from a man who was living far from God, God filled the hollow place in my heart by enlightening me to his complete joy and filling me with hope by pouring his love into my heart by the power of the Holy Spirit. The cultivation of my inner being was beginning.

Next, my heart needed a reality check about my true identity in Christ, which was absolutely essential to my success at living the Christian life, according to Neil Anderson. He pointed out how Satan was deceiving my thoughts and heart. "A Christian, in terms of our deepest identity, is a saint, a spiritually born child of God, a divine masterpiece, a child of light, a citizen of heaven. Being born again transformed you into someone who didn't exist before…. It's not what you do as a Christian that determines who you are; it's who you are that determines what you do…. The outer change of a believer's daily walk…continues throughout life."[9] My true identity in Christ was the *status change*, through Christ's death for my sins, before God. With that status change there came the responsibility to focus on cultivating my inner garden so that *who* I was in Christ reflected what I *did* as a believer in my daily walk.

With prayer, Scripture, help from Bible scholars, and my last counselor, I put on the armor of God, the armor of light (Rom. 13:12), the armor of love for battle against the spiritual forces of darkness, and prayed in the Spirit at all times (Eph. 6:10–18). I trusted in Christ's promise that God's enduring forgiving love, through the grace offered in Christ, would uphold and strengthen me as I freely confessed each sin. God already knew each of my sins. He wanted me to know each sin, as well, so that I could find joy, peace and rest in his abounding grace and enduring forgiving love.

The Holy Spirit developed my garden that Gordon MacDonald calls, "a place of potential peace and tranquility...where the Spirit of God comes to make self-disclosure, to share wisdom, to give affirmation or rebuke, to provide encouragement, and to give direction and guidance.... God does not often walk in disordered gardens."[10]

When Jesus called woes on the Pharisees, he said, "First clean the inside of the cup and dish, and then the outside also will be clean" (Matt. 23:25–26). We must be so careful not to develop a hypocritical attitude like the Pharisees. Jesus warned his disciples of this in Matthew 16:6: "Be careful.... Be on your guard against the yeast [teaching] of the Pharisees and Sadducees." Instead, submit to the Holy Spirit's inward cleansing and renewal. Walk as Christ did during his suffering and obedience to his Father. "Arm yourselves also with the same attitude, because he who has suffered in his body is done with sin. As a result, he does not live the rest of his earthly life for evil human desire, but rather for the will of God" (1 Pet. 4:1, 2).

The Israelites forgot God's love over and over as they slid into the ways of the evil nations around them and disobeyed the Father's instructions in Deuteronomy 6 on how they were to trust his love and practice it with their fellow man. Paul told us that the Israelites' experiences were for us: "These things happened to them as examples and were written down as warnings for us on whom the fulfillment of the ages has come. So, if you think you are standing firm, be careful that you don't fall" (1 Cor. 10:11–12).

As you read this book, keep in mind these words of William Kirwan, "The astonishing truth is that Jesus sees to the core of each of us and declares us of infinite worth. No part of our heart escapes His sight or His sanctifying power.... His love is all-inclusive; it accepts the whole of each of us."[11]

QUESTIONS FOR THOUGHT

1. How well do you know the Person of the Holy Spirit and the power of his ministry?

2. How important is the evidence and development of the fruit of the Holy Spirit in your life?

3. What does it mean to you when you hear that you are a temple of the Holy Spirit?

4. If you were describing your true identity in Christ to someone, how would you do that?

5. How are you cultivating your inner garden to make it resemble Christ?

6. How would your daily walk with Christ match *who* you are or what you *do* according to Christ's mandates?

CHAPTER 2

WITHOUT LOVE, NOTHING

PAUL REBUKED THE Corinthian church in his first letter because they were wandering away from their "testimony about Christ," confirmed in them before he left. They remained infants in the gospel of Christ and were unable to receive his instructions that contained the solid food they needed to bring them to maturity. They were listening to the lies of others, a gospel not of Christ, and straying into inner darkness—a knowledge about Christ but not as Paul had taught them (see 1 Cor. 1:6; 3:2–10). He had to begin his instructions all over again and rebuke them for the many ways they were being deceived: in their dependence on knowledge, their faith without love, their reliance on spiritual gifts, and the difference between speaking in tongues, gifts of prophecy, gifts to the poor, and the surrender of their bodies to the flames without love. They gained nothing because they failed to enlighten their eyes and know better the power of the Holy Spirit in them, who manifests belief and hope in Christ's love (1 Cor. 13:1–3, 13).

God uses Paul's warnings and instructions to the Corinthian church to teach us Christians not to live in futility or darkness in our understanding of the Holy Spirit who manifests Christ's love in us. We live in ignorance and our hearts slowly harden when we separate ourselves from the Holy Spirit and the life he desires for us. We were taught to put off our old self, "which is being corrupted by its deceitful desires; to be made new in the attitude of our minds; and to put on the new self, created to be like God in true righteousness and holiness" (Eph. 4:20–24). We must be aware that our behavior, both verbal and non-verbal, will prove one way or the other whether we truly know him and whether the truth about his love and forgiveness is an essential part of that knowledge. Our heart, soul, and mind must be filled with Christ's love so that our walk will adhere "to the measure of all the fullness of God" (Eph. 3:19).

The ways in which Christians walk reveal whether we are on the narrow road that leads to heaven or on the wide road that leads to hell. A new attitude in Christ can be seen in all facets of life, from childhood into adulthood, in marriage and parenting, and in our relationships with God and others. It shows in our conduct and countenance. It is not superficial or based on our works, but rooted firmly in Christ's forgiving, enduring love. Therefore, we must encourage each other daily, so that none of us is hardened by sin's deceitfulness (see Heb. 3:13).

Christ's attitude *in* us (Phil. 2:5) doesn't mean only treating people well, giving money to the poor, going to church, or being helpful to neighbors. It means that in every way, we strive to reflect Christ's character—humbleness and gentleness—the fruit of the Holy Spirit: love, joy, peace, patience, kindness, goodness, faithfulness, gentleness, and self-control (Gal. 5:22–23). When the fruit of the Spirit flows through us, we will not allow the sins of rudeness, boasting, pride, envy, anger, selfishness, and keeping a record of wrongs or delighting in evil.

Even though I was raised in a Bible-believing, Christian home and church, the practical discipleship of the fruit of the Spirit all bound together with love so that we could become more Christ-like, was missing. I heard it mentioned from time to time but not with any sense of urgency, importance, or priority. When the church neglects the discipleship of the fruit of the Spirit, love inadvertently is left up to the home. Thankfully, some parents teach true biblical love, but many do not. Often, those who do not, teach love from their own experiences, and their experiences are often contrary to biblical love.

Drs. Robert Hemfelt, Frank Minirth, and Paul Meier describe the correct and incorrect model of love using heart love tanks. The description below is an incorrect love tank, which impoverishes the parent and the child.

> If that primal need for love is not met—they carry the scars for life.... In order to keep the parents' tanks filled, there must be a consistently nurturing relationship between them.... So what if the parents are at odds, you say, as long as they can adequately love the child? The point is, unless they are keeping each other's tanks replenished, they *cannot* adequately pass a filled tank to their child. In fact, parental friction often engenders a particularly sad situation. Without realizing it, one or both parents may reverse the flow. To meet their own innate needs they draw from the child's tank what little he or she has, leaving the child with less than nothing.[1]

When the cycle flows from God to the parents to the children, then children are full of all the love they need. Sadly—as Hemfelt, Minirth, and Meier point out—the correct model is often lacking, just as I discovered during my childhood and my marriage. In both instances, I had to overcome expectations, criticism, and conditional love.

That's not to say that Christians aren't looking for the right answers about love. Larry Crabb explains that many Christians search for answers in psychology and preaching, but psychologists fail to direct them to Christ and preachers fill their members with more and more knowledge. As a consequence, "there is no legitimate separation between the academic, the devotional, and the practical study of Scripture.... Scores of people today are caught up in a superficial and distorted version of what it means to trust the Lord."[2]

That is the world I found myself in for far too long until God brought a counselor into my life who directed me to the power of the Holy Spirit, the living Christ, and his perfect love.

KNOWLEDGE WITH LOVE

Andrew Murray explains how a person may walk in a way that seems right to him or her, but in the end it leads to death (see Prov. 16:25). "We know it is possible for a man to be suffering from a disease without knowing it. What he believes to be a slight ailment turns out to be quite dangerous. Do not let us be too sure that we are not, to a large extent, still living *under the law* while considering ourselves to be living wholly *under grace*' (Rom. 6:14)."[3] The grace of Christ is his unfailing, forgiving love, evidenced on the cross and imparted to us who believe, then commanded to imitate (see Eph. 5:1–2).

Jesus rebuked the Pharisees when they taught and practiced only lip service. "You diligently study the Scriptures because you think that by them you possess eternal life. These are the Scriptures that testify about me, yet you refuse to come to me to have life.... I know that you do not have the love of God in your hearts" (John 5:39–42). We also need a rebuke from Jesus when we are content with just head knowledge, ignore the power of the Holy Spirit, have the false notion that we can ignore God's moral law, live the way that fits our head knowledge, and assume this type of life will lead us to heaven.

Even though my journey to love led me to discover my true identity in Christ and how much he loved me, I sensed that something was missing. After much prayer, God's answer again came through Andrew Murray—a prayer-filled man who wrote eloquently about our vital and abiding relationship with Jesus Christ. He said, "God's forgiving nature, revealed to us in His love, becomes our nature. With the power of His forgiving love dwelling in us, we forgive just as He forgives.... The spirit of forgiveness is the spirit of love."[4]

Of course! I was missing the close connection between *love and forgiveness*. Love is not biblical love unless it is given to all with an attitude of forgiveness, and not the other way around. After mulling over the two concepts, I realized it is impossible to love first and then to forgive. Now that I see the difference, this all-important truth jumps out of every page of the Bible and it has dramatically changed my reading and study of it. Charles Stanley puts this truth in perspective:

> Don't tell me that you love another person, but you are unwilling to talk to that person. Don't tell me that you love another person, but you just can't open up and be transparent about your feelings, ideas, or your past experiences. Don't tell me that you love another person, but you are unwilling to work on getting to the core issue of a problem that exists between you. Any time you say, "I love her, *but...*" or "I love him *when...*" you have just told me that you don't really love that person or value that relationship. The words *but*, *if*, and *when* insert conditions into a relationship, and genuine love is unconditional.[5]

What a marvelous insight! When we read with this truth in mind, we notice that Jesus spoke more about forgiveness than He did about love. The LORD's Prayer is centered on forgiveness (see Matt. 6:5–15). His model for relationships is centered on forgiveness. When Peter asked, "How many times shall I forgive," Jesus replied, "Seventy-seven times" (see Matt. 18:21–22), every time your brother repents (see Luke 17:3), and even before he might repent (see Matt. 18:15). Our forgiving love is evidenced in how we share our possessions, in how we speak and act in truth (see 1 John 3:16–22), in our marriage relationships (see 1 Pet. 3:7), and in unity with other Christians (see Col. 3:10–17). A forgiving heart grants us what we ask of God (see 1 John 3:22).

The Bible says that in marriage relationships, the spouses need to *know* each other and that degree of intimacy is how we need to know God. Intimacy with forgiving love also helps us deal with the conflicts that are part of any relationship, whether with God or our fellowman. According to David Augsburger, "Conflict is natural, normal, neutral, and sometimes even delightful. It can turn into painful or disastrous ends, but it doesn't need to. Conflict is neither good nor bad, right nor wrong. Conflict simply is. How we view, approach and work through our differences does—to a large extent—determine our whole life pattern."[6] Listening with open hearts to each other, bearing with each other, and forgiving each other, during every conflict, brings the needed healing and increases our intimacy while binding us in perfect unity with the body of Christ.

To resolve my misunderstanding about love, my first counselor advised me to stand in front of a mirror every day and say, "God loves me and I love me." As I practiced this phrase, the Holy Spirit helped me understand how I had misconstrued my concept of God and his attitude toward me, but the continual reading and studying of his Word brought that message from my head to my heart. My eyes and heart were enlightened when I saw his enduring, unfailing, forgiving love with his people Israel. Then, the message grew as I experienced the loving attitude and actions of those whom Christ empowered.

These promises from Scripture became my daily food:

"I have loved you with an everlasting love."

(Jer. 31:3)

Trust in the LORD with all your heart and lean not on your own understanding; in all your ways acknowledge him, and he will make your paths straight.

(Prov. 3:5–6)

You will keep in perfect peace him whose mind is steadfast, because he trusts in you.

(Isa. 26:3)

"Come to me, all you who are weary and burdened, and I will give you rest. Take my yoke upon you and learn from me, for I am gentle and humble in heart, and you will find rest for your souls. For my yoke is easy and my burden is light."

(Matt. 11:28–30)

These mind-changing promises slowly turned my unloving character into a deeper awareness of what it means to be gentle and humble in heart.

KNOWLEDGE WITH OBEDIENCE

Until this point, my character was suffering from the neglect of the Scriptures. When I repented and obeyed his commands, my life began to turn around. I began a life of discovery. My obedience opened the door to trust once I understood God's love and justice. We falter if we don't recognize God's hatred of every sin and his call to repentance for each sin. His balanced justice and love was demonstrated in that, "While we were still sinners, Christ died for us" (Rom. 5:8). Thus, the Holy Spirit, Scripture, obedience, gratitude, love, and forgiveness in Christ offers us this: "Whoever drinks the water I give him will never thirst. Indeed, the water I give him will become in him a spring of water welling up to eternal life" (John 4:14).

During my childhood, the messages of justice, not love, as well as emphasis on rules, was the main message of the church, which carried over into our home. Today, an imbalanced message is still evident, but from the other extreme—mostly permissive love, but little justice. According to David Henderson, "When self-absorbed, individualistic consumers and spectators move beyond God, beyond right and wrong, and beyond meaning and purpose, then what becomes of the spiritual life? It undergoes a bizarre twist and eventually gets reduced to this: I will do whatever works for me until I find something better. And God, uh.... God, umm...well, I'm not quite sure how God fits into the picture."[7]

This balanced teaching of love and justice comes through his moral law of love (the Ten Commandments). The first four are God's standards for loving him—the last six are his standards for loving one another (see Ex. 20). If for some reason this moral law doesn't seem important, we necessarily neglect their expansion in the Sermon on the Mount (see Matt. 5–7) where Jesus fulfilled them (see Matt. 5:17) and summarized them:

> "'Love the Lord your God with all your heart and with all your soul and with all your mind.' This is the first and greatest commandment. And the second is like it: 'Love your neighbor

as yourself.' All the Law and the Prophets hang on these two commandments."

(Matt. 22:37–40)

Anyone who breaks one of the least of these commandments and teaches others to do the same will be called least in the kingdom of heaven, but whoever practices and teaches these commands will be called great in the kingdom of heaven.

(Matt. 5:19)

Chuck Colson discovered the importance of the Ten Commandments after he viewed the video series by R. C. Sproul on the holiness of God. Colson saw God's great love for humanity and wondered about his own response as well as other Christians, so he did a survey. "The cumulative effect of my survey convinced me that most of us, as professing Christians, do not really know how to love God. Not only have we not given thought to what the greatest commandment means in our day-to-day existence, we have not obeyed it. And if this was true for individual believers, what were the ramifications for the church? Perhaps the reason the church was so ineffective in the world was that it had the same needs I did."[8]

I believe 1 Corinthians 13 and Galatians 5:22–26 add to the Ten Commandments a balanced message of God's love and justice. Both passages list God's evidence of love in life and the consequences if we fail to obey his commands. Walking and living in Christ's forgiving love and the fruit of the Spirit matures and prepares us on earth for heaven where prophecy and head knowledge will cease. Do we think it's necessary to take all this seriously? Revelations 1–3 indicates the seriousness of obedience to both people and churches. They are held responsible! After each admonition and encouragement, Jesus said, "He who has an ear, let him hear what the Spirit says to the churches...." Then different rewards are stated, when, and if, the church obeys.

We are warned in Scripture not to follow the disobedience of the Israelites (see 1 Cor. 10:1–13) and to be careful that we don't fall. We must not follow the teaching of the Pharisees, either, who looked "beautiful on the outside but on the inside" were "full of dead men's bones" (Matt. 16:11–12; 23:27). We should hold fast to our first love (see Rev. 2:4) while dying to the world (see John 12:24–26). Paul reminds us that, after Christ's death, God's law was placed in our hearts through the Holy Spirit's testimony (see Heb. 10:16) to make us "conscious of sin" (Rom. 3:20), and then our love for others will fulfill that law of love (Rom. 13:8–10; Gal. 5:14).

It is my belief that neglecting the teaching and practice of true biblical love as found in 1 Corinthians 13 is sinful. Our conscious mind knows the difference. Satan likes to see a Christian who possesses great head knowledge, but is lacking in love. "For the sinful nature desires what is contrary to the Spirit, and the Spirit what is contrary to the sinful nature. They are in conflict with each other, so that you do not do what you want" (Gal. 5:17). The only debt we can leave outstanding is our love for each other, for then we fulfill the moral law of love (see Rom. 13:8). If we neglect love, we become lukewarm like the church of Laodicea that Jesus spit out. Yet, he gave this assurance. "Those whom I love I rebuke and discipline. So be earnest, and repent. Here I am! I stand at the door and knock. If anyone hears my voice and opens the door, I will come in and eat with him, and he with me" (Rev. 3:19–20).

QUESTIONS FOR THOUGHT

1. In what ways does your life resemble the Corinthian church?

2. When you examine your life, where do you stand in regard to mere infancy in Christ and solid food? How would you define your head knowledge in comparison to heart knowledge?

3. How much do you know and how much searching have you done to gather the biblical truth about love?

4. How important is, and how much do you know, about God's balanced justice and love?

5. Describe the importance of your obedience to Christ seen in your walk with him.

6. What streams of living water are flowing from within you?

7. How does your life measure up with the moral law of love—the Ten Commandments?

CHAPTER 3

LOVE HAS PATIENCE
AND IS PATIENT

THE PHRASE "LOVE has patience" comes from the *Interlinear Bible* and I like it because it carries a deeper meaning than simply "love is patient." "Has" means "before" whereas "is," according to Webster, means "to be." So, an individual who has a loving attitude of patience firmly planted in Christ is someone who is already practicing patience and will continue being patient. In John 15:8 Jesus pointed out that our love and fruit reveal whether we are his disciples or not. Our obedience shows that we are clothed with patience.

Patience for a Christian is not an option, it's one of the foundations needed in order to practice any of the other love principles. It is "a determination of the will...an essential Christian virtue.... It is reliance on God and acceptance of His will, with trust in His goodness, wisdom and faithfulness."[1] Our attitude toward our practice of patience, then, will be a decision of *has* (before) and *is* (to be), not one of indifference. Oswald Chambers warns, "Beware of the danger of relaxation spiritually.... If we make our inability a barrier to obedience, it means we are telling God there is something He has not taken into account."[2]

Before we go on, let's clarify the difference between patience, endurance, and perseverance; often they are used interchangeably in the Bible. Perseverance will be considered in a later chapter. *The Bible Dictionary* says, "Two Greek words are translated by our English word *patience*, but they are not exactly synonymous in meaning. One (perseverance) is the quality of endurance under trials. It is mainly an attitude of the heart with respect to things. The other word, *longsuffering* (KJV) (or *patience*, NIV) is an attitude with respect to people.... Both terms are used of God." Webster calls perseverance a "continued patient effort," "the quality of one who perseveres," "steadfast in purpose."

The Father, Son, and Holy Spirit fit the perfect model of patience. All three were present at the time of creation. Christ perfectly obeyed the Father when he carried out his Father's will on earth. The Holy Spirit carries out God's patient work within us.

We must practice patience in two very important parts of our lives, our patience with God and our patience with others. Patience with God comes only when we have complete trust in his plan and purpose for us, shown by his love and his discipline. The deepness of our trust for God as he works out that purpose will show in our actions and words. God's plan and purpose for us is often different than the plans we want or choose for ourselves, which might cause impatience and is exhibited when we whine, complain, or ask "Why?" rather than "What can I learn from this situation where God has placed me?"

Jerry Bridges adds an excellent point regarding patience and trust:

> Sometimes our anxiousness to know the will of God comes from a desire to "peer over God's shoulder" to see what His plan is. What we need to do is learn to trust Him to guide us. Of course, this does not mean that we put our minds into neutral and expect God to guide us in some mysterious way apart from hard and prayerful thinking on our part.... In Galatians 5:22–23, the first four traits—love, joy, peace, and patience—can only be developed in the womb of adversity. We may think we have true Christian love until someone offends us or treats us unjustly.... Adversities spoil our peace and sorely try our patience. God uses those difficulties to reveal to us our need to grow, so that we will

reach out to Him to change us more and more into the likeness of His Son.[3]

When Paul described Jesus' willingness to leave heaven and come to earth to take on a human nature and humbly suffer for us, he began with if/then clauses that call us to take a good look at ourselves. He is also serious in this instruction, "Therefore…as you have always obeyed—…continue to work out your salvation with fear and trembling, for it is God who works in you to will and to act according to his good purpose. Do everything without complaining or arguing, so that you may become blameless and pure, children of God without fault in a crooked and depraved generation, in which you shine like stars in the universe as you hold out the word of life" (Phil. 2:12–16).

Paul's experiences qualify him to teach us patience as a necessary Christian virtue, for he suffered many adversities:

> We have this treasure in jars of clay to show that this *all-surpassing power is from God and not from us.* We are hard pressed on every side, but not crushed; perplexed, but not in despair; persecuted, but not abandoned; struck down, but not destroyed. We always carry around in our body the death of Jesus, so that the life of Jesus may also be revealed in our body…. Therefore we do not lose heart. Though outwardly we are wasting away, yet inwardly we are being renewed day by day. For our light and momentary troubles are achieving for us an eternal glory that far outweighs them all.
>
> (2 Cor. 4:7–11, 16–17)

The Book of James speaks much about the building and practice of patience. He not only calls us to practice patience, but to "Consider it *pure joy*" when we face different trials. Joy can be found in our tested trials of faith, when we remember the reason trials come. Our patience or perseverance, depending on the Bible version, during these times of trial, lead us to maturity and completeness, so we lack *nothing.* Both the practice of patience or perseverance and our joy is rooted in Christ, *not* in the trial. James

THE ARMOR OF LOVE

also points out that wisdom from God enables our patience and joy, and without wisdom, we are unstable (see James 1:2–8).

James begins his book with instructions about the practice of patience and he ends it that way as well. In James 5:7–11, he tells us we need to "be patient" and to "stand firm" until the LORD returns and not to "grumble against each other." Then he turns us toward the prophets "who spoke in the name of the Lord." These men endured many hardships and God asked them to perform difficult roles to show the Israelites how God viewed their disobedience. When the Israelites entered Canaan, they made this promise to Joshua: "We too will serve the LORD, because he is our God" (Josh. 24:18). Yet they repeatedly imitated the wicked nations around them. They forgot God unless they had a God-filled leader. James is correct—we can learn from the prophets.

Moses, who grew up in Pharaoh's palace, took care of sheep in the desert and then led complaining and grumbling Israelites for 40 years. There was no prophet in Israel like Moses, "whom the LORD knew face to face" (Deut. 34:10), nor one as "humble" (Num. 12:3). Jeremiah was a prophet to disobedient Judah, who answered God's call like Moses, saying he didn't know how to speak, yet God gave him the words, and he said to Jeremiah, "Get yourself ready! Stand up and say to them whatever I command you" (Jer. 1:17).

Isaiah was a spirit-filled prophet for at least 40 years. After God allowed Isaiah a glimpse of heaven and took away his sin and guilt by touching his mouth with live coals, then he called him to be his prophet (Isa. 6:1–13). He proclaimed God's sovereignty and love and he foretold Christ's birth and his agony on the cross. Isaiah revealed God's justice against the nations, Judah, and Jerusalem for their disobedience. In his role as prophet, he had to walk barefoot and naked for three years (Isa. 20:3). He also brought comfort: "The LORD is the everlasting God.... He will not grow tired or weary, and his understanding no one can fathom. He gives strength to the weary and increases the power of the weak.... Those who hope in the LORD will renew their strength. They will soar on wings like eagles; they will run and not grow weary, they will walk and not be faint" (Isa. 40:28–29, 31).

Ezekiel was called to be a watchman to the rebellious Israelites. If he didn't say what God told him to say, he would be held accountable for Israel's blood, but if he obeyed, he would save himself. Ezekiel role-played much of the LORD's instructions. He was commanded to lie on his left side for three hundred and ninety days for Israel and on his right side forty days for Judah, tied up with ropes unable to turn from side to side, bearing the sin of each nation. He also was not allowed to mourn openly when God took his wife (see Ezek. 4, 24).

The prophet Habakkuk pleaded with God to take action against the injustice of Judah. However, God told Habakkuk to trust him regardless of the circumstances and wait. "The revelation awaits an appointed time; it speaks of the end and will not prove false. *Though it linger, wait for it*; it will certainly come and will not delay" (Hab. 2:3). Habakkuk's response shows us the benefit of patience even when we don't understand:

> Though the fig tree does not bud and there are no grapes on the vines, though the olive crop fails and the fields produce no food, though there are no sheep in the pen and no cattle in the stalls, yet I will rejoice in the LORD, I will be joyful in God my Savior. The Sovereign LORD is my strength; he makes my feet like the feet of a deer, he enables me to go on the heights.
>
> (Hab. 3:17–19)

Job wasn't really a prophet, but he certainly exhibited patience. He had to learn patience with his friends and patience toward God. Job questioned God's justice and cried out to him to explain the reason behind his suffering (see Job 19:7). Even though God never explained to Job why he suffered, he honored him with a response that pointed out his sovereignty, proving God's perfect love and justice (see Job 40:2, 8; 41:11). God's answer brought Job into a greater understanding of his justice; an awareness of his great need of patience with God and that God honored his patience with his friends.

Finally, we see Jesus, the greatest prophet of all, who waited patiently since the creation of the world until "the time had fully come" to redeem us (Gal. 4:4). Now he waits, and so do we, for his final return: "He must remain in heaven until the time comes for God to restore everything, as he promised long ago through his holy prophets" (Acts 3:21).

The most important lesson we learn about patience from these great prophets and God's love and justice is that they were fighting a battle, for God against evil. Our training in patience is also a battle against the evil rulers, forces, and powers of this world (see Eph. 6:12). Once we have our patience and joy rooted in God, firmly trust in him, know our true identity in Christ and have a complete reliance on the power of the Holy Spirit, then we are fully equipped to withstand evil and practice patience with each other.

To learn and practice patience with others is one of the basic foundations of the love principles. The *Greek Interlinear Bible* says, "love *has* patience" and it is "an essential Christian virtue." We need to search our inner heart, mind, emotions, and soul to renounce any sin or stumbling block that would hinder that development. Patience is a gift of the Holy Spirit and involves our humble prayer: "Search me, O God, and know my heart; test me and know my anxious thoughts. See if there is any offensive way in me, and lead me in the way everlasting" (Ps. 139:23–24). Our commitment must be genuine and we need to be prepared to fail, for we will often stumble and stray back to our old ways, especially at first, yet our LORD waits to welcome us back, so that he can continue to work his "has patience" "is patient" position in us.

A daily stillness to cultivate, shape, and transform our lives is also required in order to build the foundation of patience. Stillness means, "to slacken, mend, heal, repair, and make whole" (*Strong's*). As Andrew Murray says, "It is when the soul is hushed in silent awe and worship before the Holy Presence that reveals itself within, that the still small voice of the blessed Spirit will be heard."[4] A soul, quiet before God, with the strength of the Holy Spirit, always knows, always waits patiently, and always trusts God's promises.

Part of our stillness before God involves meditation and what we refer to as "devotions." Two varying thoughts exist today about them. According to E. M. Bounds, "Hurried devotions make weak

faith, feeble convictions, questionable piety. To be little with God
is to be little for God. To cut short the praying makes the whole
religious character short, stingy, miserly, and slovenly.... Short
devotions cut the pipe of God's full flow. It takes time in the secret
places to get the full revelation of God. Little time and hurry mar
the picture."[5]
Here's what J. I. Packer says:

> Meditation is the activity of calling to mind, and thinking over,
> and dwelling on, and applying to oneself, the various things that
> one knows about the works and ways and purposes and promises
> of God. It is an activity of holy thought, consciously performed in
> the presence of God, under the eye of God, by the help of God,
> as a means of communion with God. Its purpose is to clear one's
> mental and spiritual vision of God, and to let His truth make its
> full and proper impact on one's mind and heart. It is a matter of
> talking to oneself about God and oneself; it is, indeed, often a
> matter of arguing with oneself, reasoning oneself out of moods
> of doubt and unbelief into a clear apprehension of God's power
> and grace. Its effect is to ever humble us as we contemplate God's
> greatness and glory, and our own littleness and sinfulness and to
> encourage and reassure us—'comfort' us in the old, strong Bible
> sense of the word—as we contemplate the unsearchable riches
> of divine mercy displayed in the Lord Jesus Christ.[6]

To meditate and build an inner life of stillness requires an even
greater test of our patience because it cannot be learned according
to the quick fix mentality of today. David Henderson, who speaks
about today's culture, says, "We're afraid to slow down, afraid of
what might bubble to the surface in the silence.... We want the
comfort of plunking down in front of something that won't challenge us, hound us, or expose us for who we really are."[7]
Seeing our souls thirst for God like a parched land, daily meditation on God's word gives us the nourishment that quenches our
thirst and the fertilizer to cultivate our inner garden. We become
"like a tree planted by streams of water, which yields it fruit in
season and whose leaf does not wither" (Ps. 1:3). Nourishment,
fertilizer, and meditation provide us patient stability and joy, which

enables God's word to be a lamp for our feet and a light for our path (Ps. 119:105). We now have the foundation of love required for our reciprocal relationships with God's people.

I love the way Jerry Bridges connects forgiveness with patience: "Forgiving costs us our sense of justice.... This forgiving aspect of love enables us to be patient with one another and to live at peace with one another.... If we are to grow in the grace of love, we must be ready to forgive, even at great cost to ourselves."[8]

When Jesus called Peter, he was prideful and impulsive. He had weak faith, doubt crept into his circumstances (when he walked on the water) and he lacked understanding of Jesus' three-year ministry. Jesus had to rebuke, discipline, train, shape, and exhort Peter in order to change his character. This change came privately and publicly. Three times Peter denied Jesus; three times Jesus asked Peter, "Do you love me?" Peter was hurt by the questions, but Jesus needed him to know, experience, and understand his transformation in order to teach it to others and be a rock for the church.

Paul explains well his encounter with Christ. "The grace of our Lord was poured out on me abundantly, along with the faith and love that are in Christ Jesus. Here is a trustworthy saying that deserves full acceptance: Christ Jesus came into the world to save sinners—of whom I am the worst. But for that very reason I was shown mercy so that in me, the worst of sinners, Christ Jesus might display his unlimited patience as an example for those who would believe on him and receive eternal life" (1 Tim. 1:14–16).

So we will benefit greatly if we allow the Holy Spirit to work his patience in our heart and mind, changing us as he did Peter and Paul. We need to heed the words of Oswald Chambers, "To 'wait on the Lord,' and to 'rest in the Lord,' is an indication of a healthy, holy faith, while impatience is an indication of an unhealthy, unholy unbelief. This well-centered strength, or patience, forms a prominent characteristic in the biblical revelation of God, of our Lord Jesus Christ, and of the saints."[9]

QUESTIONS FOR THOUGHT

1. How high a priority have you made patience, the first principle and foundation of love, in your life?

2. If you met a new believer tomorrow who asked you to explain the balance of God's love and justice—how would you do it?

3. How did the Old Testament prophets display patience in their dealings with the Israelites?

4. What forces of evil are present in your life and prevent you from learning about patience with God and with people?

5. On a scale of one to ten, with ten being the highest, how would you rate the quantity and the quality of time you spend meditating on what you've read in the Bible each day?

6. How do you exhibit patience in relationships with other people?

CHAPTER 4

LOVE IS KIND (GOOD)

THE SECOND PRINCIPLE, "Love is kind" is also a foundational attitude of love. It's a quality we often think we possess.
However, this may not be true, for it doesn't mean tolerance toward
others or being nice. Neither is it inherited or a natural ability.
Biblical kindness is much deeper, says *Vine's Greek Dictionary*;
it is gracious, gentle, compassionate, and humble-minded,[1] like
the attitude of Jesus (see Matt. 11:29). Genuine loving kindness
or goodness exhibits every fruit of the Holy Spirit with reliance
on his power. If all these qualities are not present when we think
we're expressing kindness, we are probably filling our own personal
selfish desires (see Rom. 12:1–3, 9–10).

According to Jerry Bridges, kindness and goodness "are
so closely related that they are often used interchangeably....
*Kindness is a sincere desire for the happiness of others; goodness is the
activity calculated to advance that happiness.* Kindness is the inner
disposition created by the Holy Spirit that causes us to be sensitive
to the needs of others, whether physical, emotional, or spiritual.
Goodness is kindness in action—words and deeds." Bridges adds
that, "Gentleness is...the recognition that the human personality is
valuable but fragile, and must be handled with care" and humility
"is the soil in which the other traits of the fruit of the Spirit grow."[2]

The soil is humility. I believe the *key* that effects that change in our inner disposition is the acceptance and practice of the non-separation of love and forgiveness. We give this forgiving love with the same undeserved favor that God imputed his grace (see Eph. 2:4–10). There is more. When we bestow God's grace, it must always be given with an attitude of thankfulness to him for his gift. Gratitude to God reveals our wish to *live in* his "righteousness, peace and joy" while making "every effort to *do* what leads to peace and to mutual edification" (Rom. 14:17, 19).

We don't automatically evidence all the fruit or receive an immediate change of character when the gift of the Holy Spirit comes into our heart. The acceptance of the non-separation of love and forgiveness, with a gentle and humble heart, also means a full surrender of our selfish natures to God and his commands in Scripture. This surrender involves complete trust, faithful patience, and full assurance that obedience of God's word, through the power of the Holy Spirit, will guide us in the truth. "For God did not give us a spirit of timidity, but a spirit of power, and of love and of self-discipline" (2 Tim. 1:7). According to Andrew Murray:

> As we seek to humble ourselves and renounce all wishes and all hopes of being or doing good by our own powers, God's Spirit will cause the power of Christ's death and victory over sin to work in us. As we yield all our human abilities and energies in the confession that they are nothing but sinful and worthy of death, we will die with Him, and with Him we will be raised in *"newness of Life"* (Rom. 6:4). This new life will be the little child that receives the kingdom.... Let the first work of the Holy Spirit be to humble you deep down in the very dust, so that your whole life will be a tender, brokenhearted waiting on God, in the consciousness of mercy coming from above.[3]

Before we address the positive characteristics of kindness, let's identify what prevents it. A double-bind lifestyle does not create kindness. We may not know what this term means. I didn't either until my counselor explained to me that I was raised in that kind of home. Webster says, it's, "a situation in which a person is faced

Crossroad
BIBLE INSTITUTE

P.O. Box 900
Grand Rapids, MI
49509-0900

Congratulations! Here is your complimentary book.

We'd love to hear from you after you finish reading it. Please write us and share your thoughts with us regarding this book. Please tell us what you have learned from it, how you can relate it to your life, and any additional thoughts you would like us to know.

Thanks for your input. It is valued!

Name: _____ Date: _____

ID#: _____

T1 Armor

with contradictory demands or expectations so that any action taken will appear to be wrong." My counselor identified it with the phrase, "saying one thing and doing another."

When I heard the meaning of a double-bind lifestyle, it was as if a light came on, because it always seemed as though I was doing something wrong. I believe this lifestyle could also be related to the statement we often hear when people point out that Christians don't "walk the talk." A double-bind lifestyle creates confusion in the minds of others and not kindness, goodness, humility, or gentleness. I would add that the person who lives that way is also confused.

Archibald Hart says, "Since we are responsible for our own lives and will eventually give an account to God, we cannot allow others to determine our beliefs, actions, or feelings.... Of course, this is not easy. We are conditioned by our need to please others, and we easily surrender control to them.... Reality thinking...requires us to take control of our own destiny, actions, and reactions. This way we can feel free to do what we believe God wants us to do, not in blatant disregard for the feelings of others, but in a spirit of gentleness and kindness."[4]

Kindness/goodness is not phoniness, which is similar to a double-bind lifestyle. Les Carter says, "The person who becomes committed to a particular outward image can be entrapped by it to the extent that his inward feelings are inconsistent with that image." Under his headline about controlling phoniness, Carter tells this shared story, from a farmer:

> He described himself as having been religious without being spiritual. By this he meant that he had always tried to live a moral "Christian" life but had never focused very intently on the person of God. But as he grew older he began looking into the Bible, trying to find the real purpose of life. Specifically, he studied the gospel accounts of Jesus' interactions with common folk like himself. Through his study he came to realize that while he had always acknowledged God's love intellectually, he had never pondered it deeply enough to experience it. In the twilight of his life, this old farmer dedicated himself to study and learn all he

could about the love of God. And he then committed himself to live it in such a way that others, too, could know that love.[5]

The turning point in this farmer's life was his commitment to live so others could know God's love. That's our purpose, also. I discovered that I could detect phoniness when I looked in a person's eyes and observed his or her stance—the cross of the arms or the lift of the head, even the invasion of the space of others. After my divorce, a friend of my ex-husband and me pointed out that he wondered if my defensive stance was why my ex-husband didn't believe me when I said I was sorry for my actions. Our friend was partially right. I was sorry, but phony, in that my husband's anger and the distance he put between us bothered me more.

There are many other attitudes that reflect unkindness: denial, flattery, false encouragement, an unwillingness to work through conflict, lack of honesty, a lack of thankfulness, every type of miscommunication—monologue instead of dialogue—not having an openness to integrate other peoples ideas or thoughts, showing an attitude of self-righteousness, an authoritarian attitude instead of one that is authoritative, gossip, a refusal to learn from others— an un-teachable character, any perfectionist tendencies, and our listening skills.

My training as a Stephen's Minister taught me better listening skills. We are *not* listening when: our attention is elsewhere when someone speaks to us; we interrupt and turn the conversation back to us because of something that was said; we don't encourage the one speaking to keep talking; or we excuse ourselves because we would rather be talking to someone else. Listening *is* kindness when we lean slightly forward, focus eye to eye, ask questions and comment on what they tell us, and clarify what we misunderstand. If, during our conversation, we run out of time, we set another date, convenient for both, and keep it. We do what the LORD requires of us, to act justly, to love mercy, and to walk humbly with our God (see Mic. 6:8).

Jesus was advocating kindness when he said, "In everything, do to others what you would have them do to you" (Matt. 7:12).

When he looked at Peter, after his denial, it was with love and kindness. When he addressed the soldiers, the Jewish rulers, and those who crucified him, he asked his Father to forgive them because they didn't know what they were doing. When Jesus rebuked the rich young ruler for loving his riches more than following him, he "looked at him and loved him" (Mark 10:21). He washed the feet of Judas, the man who betrayed him (see John 12:2–17). He was even kind when he rebuked the Pharisees; they needed to face their evil heart.

As we turn to the characteristics that are required in our acts of kindness, notice how Jesus exemplified each of the following: boundaries, respect, integrity, and honor when he interacted with the people in the above paragraph.

BOUNDARIES

It is important for kindness to have healthy boundaries. They draw us into closer relationships, just like God's boundaries do with us. According to Henry Cloud and John Townsend, "God's plan is that we learn how to love." However, because of relational fears:

> We try to have secret boundaries. We withdraw passively and quietly, instead of communicating an honest *no* (emphasis mine) to someone we love. We secretly resent instead of telling someone that we are angry about how they have hurt us. Often, we will privately endure the pain of someone's irresponsibility instead of telling them how their behavior affects us and other loved ones, information that would be helpful to their soul.... A partner will secretly comply with her spouse, not offering her feelings or opinions for twenty years and then suddenly "express" her boundaries by filing for divorce. Or parents will "love" their children by giving in over and over for years, not setting limits, and resenting the love they are showing. The children grow up never feeling loved, because of the lack of honesty.... An important thing to remember about boundaries is that they exist, and they will affect us, whether or not we communicate them.[6]

Stephen Covey says, "The real key to your influence with me is your example, your actual conduct. Your example flows naturally out of your character, or the kind of person you truly are—not what others say you are or what you may want me to think you are. It is evident in how I actually experience you. Your character is constantly radiating, communicating. From it, in the long run, I come to instinctively trust or distrust you and your efforts with me."[7] A kind/good disposition is what Paul would call "sound doctrine," which includes respect, self-control, sound faith, love (gentleness and humility), and endurance, integrity, honor, and soundness of speech.

RESPECT

Respect is an attitude that is crucial in all relationships. We must meet a person where he or she is and not force that person to our opinion. Webster says this means: to feel, show honor or esteem, hold in high regard, and show consideration for someone. I am positive the LORD placed me in positions, after my divorce, where I needed to learn respect when I communicated with people, a place where I was not comfortable, because of my aggressiveness. The positions were: a cashier, interior design receptionist, supervisor of inventory control for several sales people—in a team environment, and phone conversations as a volunteer coordinator. All these positions involved close associations.

Respect in relationships starts with respect for oneself in Christ. My last counselor kept telling me to respect that child within me, which meant treating myself with the same mercy, kindness, and forgiveness that the LORD was giving me. My divorce group co-pastor reinforced it when he said, "Your parents love you even if they don't understand how to express it." I pondered all this for some time but it came together when I read Rick Warren's words, "It doesn't matter whether your parents were good, bad, or indifferent.... God never does anything accidentally.... God's motive for creating you was his love."[8]

According to Archibald Hart, "The more you are genuinely yourself, the more you respect the rights of others. You stop pretending that you are someone you are not. You stop being afraid of not meeting the expectations of others. It's not that you don't care what they think—of course you do. You just don't let fear direct your life. You direct it yourself. That way, when you stand before God to give a full account of your life, you can do so without having to confess that you lived to please others rather than living solely to please Him."[9]

INTEGRITY

Christian kindness includes integrity. According to Andrew Murray, "There is a complaint everywhere…of the lack of a high standard of integrity and godliness, even among the professing members of Christian churches…. Think of how much there is of unlovingness [sic], temper, sharpness, and bitterness. Think how often there is strife…envy, jealousy, sensitiveness, and pride…. 'Where are marks of the presence of the Spirit of the Lamb of God?' Wanting, sadly wanting!"[10] Christians, who engage in any of these aspects of our sinful nature, radiate and communicate whether we are trustworthy or not and show the quality and degree of our love.

Psalm 15 is God's requirement for our integrity:

> LORD, who may dwell in your sanctuary? Who may live on your holy hill? He whose walk is blameless and who does what is righteous, who speaks the truth from his heart and has no slander on his tongue, who does his neighbor no wrong and casts no slur on his fellowman, who despises a vile man but honors those who fear the LORD, who keeps his oath even when it hurts, who lends his money without usury and does not accept a bribe against the innocent. He who does these things will never be shaken.

God used Job's integrity, a man who was "blameless and upright" (Job 1:8) and who feared God and shunned evil, as a tool against the devil and as a lesson for us. Job maintained his integrity even during his discourse with his three friends who accused him by saying his extreme suffering was caused by his sin. God affirmed Job when He asked Job to pray for his three friends so God's anger could be turned away from them, for they had not spoken right about God as Job did (Job 42:7–9). How quickly we hinder God's kindness when we neglect the command to be blameless, righteous, and holy.

Keep in mind that all actions of integrity involve verbal and non-verbal communication. Be careful to avoid saying one thing and doing another. As Norman Wright says, "If you are a person of integrity, you treat every person in a consistent manner by the same set of principles, whether or not they are in your presence. Integrity means you do not belittle, criticize, gossip, or betray confidences. There is no subtle or overt deception involved in what you do or say."[11] Instead, we trust in the Holy Spirit to guide us so we can build our character to imitate Christ in every part of our lives.

HONOR

The final characteristic of kindness is one of honor. However, demonstrating honor is impossible without first developing healthy boundaries, respect, and integrity. Again, Norman Wright helps us: "The Bible gives us three levels of honor…. The first level is intrinsic honor…honor possessed by God and given to every human being…. The second level is honor based on character. The third level of honor is based on performance…. Honoring another person can help to change his life, whether he wants to change or not. It's easy to honor an honorable person, but honoring the pain in the neck is another thing."[12]

Notice the elements of honor: "He who pursues righteousness and love finds life, prosperity and honor" (Prov. 21:21); "The fear of the LORD teaches a man wisdom, and humility comes before honor" (Prov. 15:33) and "Honor one another above yourselves" (Rom. 12:10). Jesus' parables and teachings provided the correct way to pursue righteousness toward honor. He relates to all his children with humbleness and honor. He is a shepherd willing to leave his flock in order to save the one who might be lost. He condemns the man who is unmerciful toward his servant even though he himself received mercy. He told us about a father who welcomed his wayward son back into the fold after a time of debauchery and a father who showed love and kindness to an angry son.

The ability to honor God or others comes only when we learn from Jesus. Learning from him comes when we meditate on his word and pray. This prayer by St. Francis of Assisi is a good place to start:

> LORD, make me an instrument of your peace.
> Where there is hatred, let me sow love;
> where there is injury, pardon;
> where there is doubt, faith;
> where there is despair, hope;
> where there is darkness, light;
> and where there is sadness, joy.
> O DIVINE MASTER,
> grant that I may not so much seek
> to be consoled as to console;
> to be understood as to understand;
> to be loved as to love;
> for it is in giving that we receive;
> it is in pardoning that we are pardoned;
> and it is in dying that we are born to eternal life.

QUESTIONS FOR THOUGHT

1. What do you find when you look inside yourself to see if kindness, goodness, gentleness, or humility is evident in all your relationships?

2. Describe your listening skills. Describe any double-bind areas and phoniness.

3. When you approach Holy Communion, does your life match Christ's character, or are you led astray by your own sinful desires?

4. How would you describe your boundaries, respect, and integrity in your relationships with others? How does your integrity line up with Psalm 15?

5. When was the last time you looked at your life, to see if you display all the levels of honor?

6. How would you describe the pursuit of righteousness and holiness in your life?

7. How solid and steadfast are you as an "instrument of peace"?

CHAPTER 5

LOVE IS NOT RUDE

W E TURN NEXT to the love principles that point out sinful attitudes and behaviors that prevent love. As Christians, we may deal with all or some of them, yet allowing any of them to remain uncontrolled in our lives will prove whether the love principles and the fruit of the Spirit are important to us and how strongly we pursue the development of a Christ-like character. If we do nothing to change these sinful principles, their continued presence shows that we depend little upon the Holy Spirit. One of the reasons I am dealing with the concept of "love is not rude" before the others is because rudeness is the direct opposite of patience and kindness/goodness.

The second reason rudeness comes next is because this sinful attitude and behavior was mine for most of my life until I became aware that if I wished to live according to the love principles, the fruit of the Spirit and dependence on the Holy Spirit, God needed to change me. Webster finds a rude person insolent, impudent, impolite, unmannerly, discourteous, uncouth, boorish, course, vulgar, rough, violent, and harsh. They lack refinement, culture, elegance, show little skill or development, and are not finished.

I carried a rude personality and a nature of defensiveness, which was offensive to others and to tell the truth, it was offensive

41

to me, too. According to Les Carter, "**Defensiveness** *is a person's resistance to personal frustration and interpersonal conflict, a protective measure which shields oneself from anxiety due to a perceived threat.*" To better understand defensiveness, I'm listing the headings of Carter's reasons for and behaviors of this problem: "The need to maintain self-esteem, fear of being vulnerable, misguided notions about anger, desire to remain in control, and the inability to admit weakness. Defensive behaviors: denying unpleasant realities, tuning out other people, transferring blame, boomeranging, taking the offensive, rationalizing, projecting, using sarcasm, fantasizing, holding stubbornly to opinions, and using passive-aggressive techniques."[1]

Even though my rudeness and defensiveness was so offensive, no one ever suggested that I needed the love principles and the fruit of the Spirit to overcome this unhealthy problem. I was generally told to stop the way I was acting or I was ignored. It was J. I. Packer's book, *Knowing God,* and Charles Swindoll's book, *Laugh Again,* about the joy found in the book of Philippians that the Holy Spirit used to start enlightening me. Then, a few years later, when I met my last counselor, she continued that enlightenment through prayer with the Holy Spirit. Even after 50 years as a Christian, when solid food should have been my steady diet, my faith was still in its infancy. Listen to these words of wisdom from Larry Crabb:

> Most modern approaches to understanding ourself and changing come back to the central ingredient of effort…. Try harder!… But God has not kept His distance. He deals with life as it is, not as we wish it were. If we desire to meet Him and to taste His loving power, we must open our eyes to whatever is true, however unsettling it may be. And it will be unsettling…. Remind yourself of what you know is true, enjoy the good things that God has given you now, and look for ways to express love to people. But remain open to confusion, disappointment, and conviction. Honor your commitment to face life honestly. Fight against defensiveness and denial…. There *is* a path to change from the inside out. Don't give up![2]

More of my lack of development came to the surface when I read Neil Anderson's book, *The Bondage Breaker*. Here I discovered that I really didn't understand my true identity in Christ. I was still walking in my old nature and listening to the lies of Satan while claiming a new nature, which was really only head knowledge. I needed heart-knowledge. To change that, I needed to study Scripture—not only learning about the holy nature of God—his sovereignty and justice, but also to apply and practice his instructions about what it meant to be a disciple and follower of Christ; to develop heart knowledge from my head knowledge and live out his gospel message.

None of this was easy for me. But then, it's not easy for anyone to take a look inside and face a dysfunctional personality or character, because we may not like what we see or do. When I first started, it seemed as though I was setting myself up for all failures. It's by the grace of God that I was led to a prayerful counselor, who knew where the power of change was found—The Holy Spirit. She helped me see that staying in the unknown because of fear of failure is denial, and that admitting I needed help was the first major step in overcoming an unhealthy lifestyle.

Besides many others, one incident that entered into my fear of failure came before I met this new counselor. I was doing daily Bible reading and study, which was good, but resulted in failure, because I didn't keep it private. I was studying openly and not with the proper attitude before my husband. I hinted that it might be helpful if he did the same thing, or that we could do it together. Needless to say, that didn't go over well. Again, my rude, impolite behavior came to the surface and my lack of loving-kindness. My unchristian behavior wasn't fully understood until I shared this incident with my new counselor, but by then we were divorced.

Yet, what happened was most helpful for my changes, because it showed my co-dependency, the need for approval, and how these things interfered with my decision to live for God. We also see my lack of communication skills—the demise of many of my relationships. If people did continue a relationship, it seemed it was because they either felt sorry for me or were able to see below the surface and knew I hated being this way. I spent a lot of time on the phone or in person, apologizing and letting people know that everything was my fault and I really didn't mean what I had said or done. It was ironic because I didn't want to admit to my weaknesses, yet the repetition of those weaknesses were evident to everyone but me, and the relationships turned sour anyway.

It took many more tries and failures, similar to those in the last two paragraphs before my relationships started to change for the better. *Vine's Greek Dictionary* explains well what was happening, "As the conscience of the believer receives enlightenment, what formerly may have been done in ignorance becomes a sin against the light and demands a special confession to receive forgiveness."[3] As the Holy Spirit brought my failures and sins to the surface, he gave me the insight, ability, and courage to accept and confess them. My responsibility was simply to be obedient to his guidance; remembering that God's love for me would not change. His faithfulness, forgiveness, and "perfect peace" stayed constant, as he replaced my false teachings and behaviors with Christ's message of love. My responsibility, again, was simply to stay steadfast and trust in him (see Is. 26:3, 4).

Another enlightenment was the discovery of some awesome words found in chapters one and two of Proverbs. Solomon said that he wrote these Proverbs "for attaining wisdom and discipline; for understanding words of insight; for...doing what is right and just and fair; for giving prudence to the simple" (Prov. 1:1–4). Then, he explains how to practice wisdom. We need to "store up," "apply," "call out" and "cry aloud" for wisdom, as if we were searching for "hidden treasure." Then, wisdom would enter our heart and knowledge will be pleasant to our soul. Discretion would protect us and understanding would guard us (see Prov. 2:1–11). Amen! What a fantastic truth. The Holy Spirit takes ignorance, harshness, and rudeness and turns it into wisdom.

RUDENESS

My rude attitudes and behaviors originated in my childhood home, but they increased as I grew older, even entering my marriage.

I'm not saying that my family never had fun, did good things for each other, or that everything in my home was a disastrous mess. Someone read the Bible after every meal, we attended church twice on Sunday, my parents provided Christian school, and the love that was taught and practiced was what my parents knew. What I am saying is that the general atmosphere of our home was quarreling, criticism, judgment, anger, a lack of forgiveness, and conditional love. Most of the discipline was spanking, hitting, yelling, or restriction of an outside activity. Even many good times carried rudeness, but that just seemed "normal." What was important was obeying all the church rules—never missing church twice on Sunday, never eating in restaurants on Sunday, no card playing, dancing, swearing, movies, drinking, etc. (see Col. 2:20–33).

Most of our family discussions were a battle to see which person would be right and which one would be wrong. We were a black and white family—no in-between. Agreeing to disagree was an unknown and we were never taught that we could learn from each other or that everyone might have had something to add to the conversation. Sarcasm was "normal" in our family, each sibling hoping to gain an edge over another sibling or even our parents, if we thought we could get away with it. Encouragement or praise was absent, and if it did come, it was often accompanied by a negative comment.

David Stoop and James Masteller describe the type of home I grew up in as a rigid family, disengaged, where there is no loyalty or closeness, an extreme lack of emotional bonding, and where the individual feels isolated. Stoop and Masteller say this type of family is the "most severely disturbed pattern of family dysfunction, and the one that has the most negative impact on its members. People from this kind of family are like isolated islands, with few (if any) personal relationships that involve any degree of attachment. Whatever relationships they *do* have are typically devoid of emotional content, existing for utilitarian purposes only."[4] My spouse, on the other hand, came from a permissive environment, which also leads to rudeness. He dealt with life by denial and running away, whereas I was taught to confront and fight.

Because of the atmosphere of rudeness in my childhood home, it is my belief that the love principles and the fruit of the Spirit either were absent by choice or were never learned. This sets the stage for the development of rudeness, impoliteness, ignorance, harsh, unskilled people, and a lack of refinement. If these behaviors were corrected, we were generally told just to behave ourselves. We were not told what "just behave" was supposed to mean. I took "just behave" to mean act like my parents and like the Christians in our neighborhood. We were not allowed to question things, but after I began this long journey, my parents were open to some of the things I tried to discuss with them, but not to others.

I believe these unskilled and undeveloped behaviors stayed prominent because we lived in denial and believed lies. These lies can transfer from generation to generation. I think the lies start in the first place when people want to cover up attitudes or characteristics they don't like to see in themselves, then eventually they use masks, thinking no one will notice. However, these masks are like the lies, that if lived for a long time become truth for that person. The problem, as we all know, is that lies, masks, and denial cannot be covered up forever. They eventually surface, and when they do, we have two choices: either continue the denial or face them. If we choose to face the denial, we again have two choices: just admit them or change them.

Dr. Chris Thurman says, "MOST OF OUR UNHAPPINESS AND EMOTIONAL STRUGGLES ARE CAUSED BY THE LIES WE TELL OURSELVES. *That* is a critically important truth.... And until we identify our lies and replace them with the truth, emotional wellbeing is impossible. Your brain is much like a tape deck.... These are tapes which hold all the beliefs, attitudes, and expectations that you have "recorded" during your life.... The longer a tape has been played, the more rigidly you believe it to be true.... Your emotional life hangs in the balance.... Both lies and truth want to control your tape deck, and whichever gains that control dictates what your life will be like."[5]

The first lie I faced, exposed by my counselor, was that of a shame-based character, a term completely unknown to me. I learned the truth about this characteristic from a cassette tape and book by John Bradshaw. Everything he said fit me perfectly. He explained the difference between healthy and unhealthy shame and guilt. Healthy shame has a boundary system of limits, direction, trust, doubt, and autonomy, which is taught to children from ages five months to three years, so they find safety. "Healthy guilt is the emotional core of our conscience. It is emotion which results from behaving in a manner contrary to our beliefs and values.... This stage begins after age three. Guilt is developmentally more mature than shame." Unhealthy shame or toxic shame can originate from one, from a mixture, or all of these: sexual, physical, emotional, and abandonment abuse.

> Toxic shame, the shame that binds you, is experienced as the all-pervasive sense that I am flawed and defective as a human being. Toxic shame is no longer an emotion that signals our limits, it is a state of being, a core identity...a rupture of the self with the self.... The characterological styles of shamelessness...include perfectionism, striving for power and control, rage, arrogance, criticism and blame, judgmentalness and moralizing, contempt, patronization, caretaking and helping, envy, people-pleasing and being nice. Each behavior focuses on another person and takes the heat off oneself.[6]

The second lie was co-dependency. Drs. Robert Hemfelt, Frank Minirth, and Paul Meier define its characteristics. It is "an addiction to people, behaviors, or things. Codependency is the fallacy of trying to control interior feelings by controlling people, things, and events on the outside.... Codependents can be like vacuum cleaners gone wild, drawing to themselves not just another person, but also chemicals (alcohol or drugs, primarily) or things—money, food, sexuality, work. They struggle relentlessly to fill the great emotional vacuum within themselves. Our patients have described it as 'Walking around feeling like the hole in the center of the doughnut. There is something missing inside me.'"[7]

The third lie was anger, which is explained fully in chapter nine. The fourth lie is perfectionism. Notice the connection to Bradshaw's "characterological styles of shamelessness." Facing perfectionism is extremely difficult to accept, admit, and change. I still battle with it at times. The truth about this damaging attitude, with its undercurrent of anger, came through reading several personal growth books by professional counselors. Rather than trying to explain it and all its characteristics, I am going to let David Seamands tell you:

> Perfectionism is a counterfeit for Christian perfection.... It walks into my office more often than any other single Christian hangup.... Its symptoms [are]: *Tyranny of the oughts....* A constant, overall feeling of never doing well enough or being good enough...especially affects our spiritual lives.... *Self-depreciation....* With increased efforts to please yourself and an increasingly demanding God who is never quite satisfied... but you must never stop trying.... *Anxiety.* The oughts and self-depreciation produce an oversensitive conscience under a giant umbrella of...condemnation.... *Legalism....* They are rigid in their outlook, frigid in their lovelessness, conforming to the approval and disapproval of others. Yet, in a strange paradox, they critically judge, blame, and bind those same others. *Anger....* A resentment against the oughts, the Christian faith, other Christians, himself, but saddest of all, against God. Oh, not that it's really against the true God...[but] a caricature of a god who is never satisfied. [And] *Denial....* Because anger is considered a terrible sin, it is pushed down.... There is only one ultimate cure for perfectionism.... Grace.... Reprogramming—the renewal of the mind that brings transformation.[8]

To transform perfectionism means admitting it to oneself over and over again every time it surfaces, because it invades a person's whole life. Charles Swindoll puts it this way, "God bless you if you're a perfectionist...and God help you! God especially help those who live with you!" Then he includes this humorous definition, "A perfectionist is one who takes great pains...and gives them to others!"[9] This is not an attitude that is conducive to lasting relationships. It will involve pain and emotional vulnerability again and again, but don't deny it. Seek healing no matter what or how much or how vulnerable you become. Spend much time in prayer, for only the Holy Spirit can help a person correct such negative training and forgive the sins that become a part of this attitude.

The fifth lie was a performance-based life. What we *do* is more important than what we *are!* Growing up, I was taught to be a people-pleaser. In my marriage, I learned to disregard what people thought. This led to inner confusion. Performance isn't the most important thing in life; it's true saving faith in Jesus Christ and then experiencing "grace transformation." When deep, true, saving faith through grace enters our lives, and our inner being is cultivated into a well-ordered garden, we have the necessary provision for a Christ-like performance lifestyle, and we will correctly manifest the Holy Spirit's gifts.

If churches, schools, and homes spent more time in inner cultivation—grace transformation, let's call it discipleship—it would decrease the need for many Christians that seek help from counselors like David Seamands for the healing of perfectionism and performance-based lives. Paul says, "Do not lie to each other, since you have taken off your old self with its practices and have put on the new self, which is being renewed in knowledge in the image of its Creator" (Col. 3:9–10). Be aware, as Dr Thurman said, "The longer a tape has been played, the more rigidly you believe it to be true."

Paul believed the lies too, until Christ brought him to his knees. He was an intelligent, knowledgeable, zealous Pharisee, "a separated one" and "loyal to God." Paul and the other Pharisees thought their knowledge of Scripture and following their manmade laws would bring them salvation (see Phil. 3:4–6). Of course, that's not true. He admits to possessing rude, ungracious, unkind behavior—a man who was unfinished. "I was once a blasphemer and a persecutor and a violent man, I was shown mercy because I acted in ignorance and unbelief" (1 Tim. 1:13). Jesus made Paul face his lies and he dramatically changed him (see Acts 9:15; Eph. 3:7–13; Gal. 1:15–16).

Joseph, I believe, was raised in an unmannerly, unrefined, un-skilled, undeveloped, ignorant, rude, and unfinished atmosphere. (Look at his brothers.) He had to be retrained to learn the correct

THE ARMOR OF LOVE

type of love. For his father "loved Joseph more than any of his other sons." Favoritism is a sin (see James 2:9; Rom. 2:11; Col. 3:25), which created a seventeen year-old child who was selfish, haughty, superior, unkind, and spoiled. We also see how Jacob learned love from his own mother and father. His mother loved him more than she loved his brother Esau, and his father Isaac loved Esau more than he loved Jacob (see Gen. 25:28). Joseph learned *about* God from Jacob, but after he was sold into slavery by his brothers (according to God's will—see Gen. 45:7), and taken to Egypt, then God taught Joseph to *know* him and ultimately that changed all of them—Joseph became a type of Christ, his brothers learned repentance, and Jacob learned to trust God (Gen. 48:15).

Paul, Joseph, and I faced the sin of rudeness, lies, anger, perfectionism, and performance, yet God was faithful throughout. The scars and memories of the past may never totally disappear, as we see in all three of our lives, but they slowly fade as we deal effectively with each one and apply grace-love transformation (see Eph. 1:7–9; Rom. 5:17).

RECOVERY

To recover from a life of rudeness, we generally need the help of a Christian counselor. If you need a counselor, please find someone who believes and trusts in the power of the Holy Spirit and who finds healing in God's Word. You may also need to find other people to support you besides a counselor. Seek all with care. A person in recovery from any of these circumstances needs understanding and empathy, not sympathy.

Keep in mind that everyone travels a different journey. What worked for one of us may not work for someone else. Also, the Holy Spirit may work with each person in different ways, and each person may be in a different phase of his or her spiritual journey. If a layperson is sought out or offers help, it's important to seek a Christian who knows what it means to be a "workman approved by God." He or she must not have a controversial attitude but one of kindness, respect, integrity, honor, and gentleness. It is helpful if both the person playing the counselor role and the counselee have teachable spirits. The helper must have boundaries so he or she in turn can teach boundaries to the person who is seeking help in the hope that God grants repentance leading to true knowledge, so no one is led astray by the trap of the devil (see 2 Tim. 2:24–26).

The LORD instructed me with His Word, but he placed others there, too: my counselor, some friends, my sister, a pastor, and most of all, books. The pastor re-parented me with unconditional love until my divorce was final and pointed me to Hebrews 12 so that I would understand how the LORD used his discipline to change me. Unfailing, forgiving love with discipline seemed unbelievable to me, because of the unloving discipline of my childhood home, but it proved true. When I truly threw off everything that hindered me and the sin that so easily entangled me, and steadfastly fixed my eyes on Jesus so that I didn't grow weary and lose heart (see Heb. 12:1–3), I discovered Christ's holiness and later a harvest of righteousness and peace (see Heb. 12:10–15).

Robert Hemfelt, Frank Minirth, and Paul Meier have ten recovery stages of co-dependency, which provided a formula to follow in changing not only my co-dependency but also the rest of the lies. I have summarized and included the actions of those ten stages for those who may wish to use them. They are: discover the truth; examine and perhaps reset your personal boundaries; find your addictions and compulsions and take steps to master them; say goodbyes, which are appropriate to healing; and when we reach the bottom—the very pit of our emotions and feelings, don't give up—it's also the start upward. Then we make new decisions, build a new foundation to bolster new decisions, rebuild our past, the present, and the future, find new and refreshed relationships, and maintain this program for the remainder of our lives.[10]

Once we are on the road to recovery, the most important step is to determine our true relationship, value, and identity in Christ. He has created our innermost being. He knows everything about us, even when we try to hide in the dark, for darkness is as light to him (see Ps. 139). We must check our inner garden—our heart, soul, and mind to see how much cultivation it needs, and heed Jesus' words: "Make a tree good and its fruit will be good, or make a tree bad and its fruit will be bad, for a tree is recognized by its fruit" (Matt. 12:33). "I am the light of the world. Whoever follows me will never walk in darkness, but will have the light of life.... If you hold to my teaching, you are really my disciples. Then you will know the truth, and the truth will set you free" (John 8:12, 31–32).

The choices we make start at birth, and our behavior reflects those choices, from childhood to adulthood and beyond, no matter how they are acquired or whether they are good or bad. Even indifference is a choice. If our parents are Christians, our knowledge and walk with Christ will generally follow their faith, at least while we are children. Whether our parents are Christians or not, the Holy Spirit still works in each person's life, calling him or her to Christ through repentance, and we make the choice to follow that call or disregard it (see Mark 10:23–32).

Recovery through repentance is, "the spiritual change implied in a sinner's return to God. The term signifies 'to have another mind.' ...The change...is so deep and radical as to affect the whole spiritual nature and to involve the entire personality. The intellect must function, the emotions must be aroused, and the will must act. Psychology shows repentance to be profound, personal and all-pervasive."[11]

Not only do the first two chapters of the book of Proverbs give us excellent guidance; the rest of the book gives us "another mind," one of wisdom from a loving, kind Father who warns and instructs us. Then it ends with people of noble character. The husband shows confidence in his wife and praises her; her children call her blessed and he is respected at the city gates where he takes his seat among the elders of the land (see Prov. 31:22–31). This husband and wife have hearts filled by the love of God. They share reciprocal loving instruction and submission to one another out of reverence for Christ, and that love flows down to the child (Eph. 5:21)!

QUESTIONS FOR THOUGHT

1. In what ways do rudeness, ignorance, or lies govern your life? How did you allow those character traits to take root?

2. What areas of your life are undeveloped or untrained?

3. How do you face the lies or sin, and what steps do you take to change them?

4. How do you react when you fail, and what impact does it have on any further changes that need to be made?

5. Name one area in your life in which you fear the unknown. How does a fear of the unknown rob you of joy and peace?

6. How would you describe your true identity in Christ and how much he values you?

CHAPTER 6

LOVE DOES NOT ENVY

LOVE DOES NOT envy is a love principle that calls us to face a sin most of us would rather not deal with nor admit. Envy is a form of rudeness and may be momentary or last for long periods of time. If it's the type of envy that lasts in our minds and hearts, we have an "unordered, un-cultivated inner garden"—one that's sinful, dangerous, and hinders our relationship with Christ because envy comes directly from Satan. It is not easy to stop, once we listen and/or submit to him. According to Oswald Chambers, "Yield for one second to anything…(whether it be the lust of the flesh or the lust of the mind)—once yield and though you may hate yourself for having yielded, you are a bondslave to that thing…because you yielded to it willingly."[1]

According to the thesaurus, other synonyms of envy are jealousy, covetousness, and spitefulness. A co-worker, who went through seminary, challenged me when I related envy to covetousness, so I checked *Vine's Greek Dictionary* for the definition of envy. *Vine* associated the two. After linking the two, the dictionary also links jealousy, desire, and lust. Both envy and covetousness were terms signifying: a lusting after something, wanting more, or a wish to have what belongs to others. The only difference between envy and jealousy was this: "envy desires to deprive another of what he has, jealousy desires to have the same or the same sort of thing for itself."[2]

James helps us here, when he asks, "What causes fights and quarrels among you? Don't they come from your desires that battle within you? You want something but don't get it. You kill and covet, but you cannot have what you want. You quarrel and fight. You do not have, because you do not ask God. When you ask, you do not receive, because you ask with wrong motives, that you may spend what you get on your pleasures" (James 4:1–3). In Galatians, Paul lists the acts of our sinful nature that cause our battles, conflict, false desires, false motives, and are contrary to the Spirit. These acts include: envy, jealousy, fits of rage, and discord and they have serious consequences. "Those who live like this will not inherit the kingdom of God" (see Gal. 5:19–21).

Les Carter defines envy as, "a subtle form of anger gone awry...a feeling of resentment or discontentment about the advantages, possessions, or successes of another.... It involves bitterness and malicious thoughts.... Envy is a broad-based emotion that ruins one's emotional nature." Carter lists twenty characteristics that identify an envious nature—ten are included here. "Envious people find it easy to examine others with a critical eye, have hidden feelings of inferiority, need much overt recognition of their achievements, enjoy the feeling of being in control, tend to be status-conscious, cringe at the idea of examining their own weaknesses, find it hard to pay compliments, tend to hold grudges, base their self-image on their performance, [and] are prone to hold 'pet peeves.'"[3]

James gave us a warning about why these evil desires are present, but he adds more—saying that choosing friendship with evil or the world means "hatred toward God." The good news is that God gives us the grace to resist and flee from the devil (see James 4:4–7). When we put on the full armor of God, we are wearing his unfailing love or grace—the strength and power that turns us from our evil desires and wrong motives and enables us to stand against the devil's schemes (see Eph. 6:10–11).

Why is putting on the full armor of God so important? It is because the LORD searches every heart and understands every motive behind our thoughts (see 1 Chron. 28:9). Our thoughts reveal our hidden evil desires and show our imprisonment of them and/or if we are taken hostage to the mind of the world. Archibald Hart explains well how our thought life influences all of life. "In a nutshell: Who you are, as a Christian believer, can be no better and no worse than the thoughts you entertain in your head.... Your brain is no stronger than your weakest thought, and your character no more virtuous than your most private reflections."[4] Hart's graph shows that our thoughts:

- Form spirituality
- Shape attitudes
- Forge character
- Determine behaviors
- Influence the immune system
- Change emotions

"The activity of your mind is like a stream that flows through your consciousness.... It passes briefly through a narrow window of awareness. Then it moves on again...to influence some other part of your being. Sometimes it is a small stream...as if the mind is in neutral.... At other times, the stream is a raging torrent.... There is no relief even in sleep.... The stream of thought, then, is something we must reckon with. Unless we take control of it, it will take control of us, and it can be a demanding taskmaster. The key to controlling our emotions lies in learning how to have some influence over our stream of thought.... God will only do what we allow him to do within us."[5]

In Jesus' description of his parable about the farmer sowing seed, we see how his Word is received in our thoughts. For those who don't receive his Word, Satan takes it away. Others hear the Word and at once receive it with joy. However, since they have no root they last only a short time. When trouble or persecution comes, they quickly fall away. Still others hear the Word but the worries of this life, the deceitfulness of wealth and the desires for other things come in and choke the Word, making it unfruitful. Others hear the Word, accept it, and produce a crop—thirty, sixty, or even a hundred times what was sown (see Mark 4:3–20). Personally, my hearing of the Word matched the seed sown where the worries of this life and the desires for other things came in and choked the Word, making it unfruitful.

Hart's book, *Habits of the Mind*, clearly showed how my thoughts kept me on a downward spiral. I immediately started putting his exercises into practice so that I could keep my thoughts and emotions under the captivity of Christ. I face dangerous thoughts or evil desires now as soon as I recognize them, giving them to Christ, and I don't rationalize them at night anymore, which is another dangerous habit. I deal with them immediately, keeping in mind Paul's principle about anger, not letting the sun go down on my envious and wayward thoughts (see Eph. 4:26).

I also use a practice I learned from Larry Christenson: "Once Christ has delivered you from the power of sin and the devil, you can depend on it: that old landlord will soon come back knocking at your door.... *We don't have to let him in!* Christ has delivered us.... When these thoughts come knocking at the door of our mind, we can quietly send them on to Jesus. Don't argue with them. That's letting them get one foot in the door. (That was Eve's trouble—she got into a conversation with the tempter.) Before the conversation even gets under way, quietly and confidently say, 'Take that up with Jesus.'"[6] Do this aloud because Satan can't hear your thoughts; he only sees your actions.

We do indeed have a choice in the matter. God's instructions are:

> Get rid of all moral filth and the evil that is so prevalent and humbly accept the word planted in you, which can save you. Do not merely listen to the word, and so deceive yourselves. Do what it says. Anyone who listens to the word but does not do what it says is like a man who looks at his face in a mirror and, after looking at himself, goes away and immediately forgets what he looks like. But the man who looks intently into the perfect law

that gives freedom, and continues to do this, not forgetting what he has heard, but doing it—he will be blessed in what he does.
(James 1:21–25)

Long-term envy becomes a stronghold when we only cope with the symptoms and fail to recognize and deal with the roots of envy. The first root is discontentment. Jerry Bridges said, "The idea of contentment in the Bible is most often associated with possessions or money…. After possessions, probably the most common need is to learn contentment with our place in society or in the body of Christ…. Discontent is one of the most satanic of all sins, and to indulge in it is to rebel against God just as Satan did…. Only the Holy Spirit can work a lasting and fundamental attitude change deep in your heart, so make contentment a matter of regular, earnest prayer."[7]

Discontentment started with Adam and Eve in the garden when Satan lied to them. First, he prompted Eve to think about God's command not to eat of the tree in the middle of the garden, because they would die. Then he changed the command slightly by letting Eve think he knew God's mind about why they couldn't eat by saying, "You will not surely die." Eve listened and discontentment entered her heart. The fruit was pleasing to her eye and also desirable for gaining wisdom, so she ate and then gave some to Adam. However, Satan didn't bother to explain what would really happen—the loss of their close, innocent, non-sinful fellowship with God. Their choice to listen to Satan also resulted in fear, shame, blame, and a curse to them and all people.

The pages of Scripture in both the Old and New Testaments are very clear about the on-going discontent in the lives of the people. The experiences in my childhood home of discontent were seen through envious, critical, and unloving attitudes. I always wished that I was someone else or lived somewhere else. I disliked my personality, our repeated farm work, which kept us from having fun like our peers, and it fostered a sense of competition between my siblings and me. I was rebellious and only years later, after God tore down my many strongholds, did I learn to appreciate the blessings that were on that farm: a valuable work ethic, financial security, music abilities, exposure to a Christian school and church, and the security of family life in general.

Charles Stanley said, "If we can lose our peace and joy when our circumstances turn bad, the peace and joy we were experiencing were not fruits of the Spirit.... As long as our contentment can be destroyed by a change in our environment, we can never be content in any circumstance."[8] Paul's joy and peace stayed strong because his weapons against discontentment were God's divine power, taking every thought captive to Christ (see 2 Cor. 10:4, 5), the Holy Spirit, sincere love, and weapons of righteousness (see 2 Cor. 6:7). Our contentment, thoughts, and circumstances are all related, both positive and negative, depending on the strength or weakness of our prayer life, our attitudes, our obedience to Christ, and our thankfulness (see Phil. 4).

The second root of envy is bitterness. When we aren't satisfied with our lot in life and always desire something else, bitterness is a natural result, which the writer of Psalm 73 discovered. The opposite of peace and joy is bitterness; that's why Hebrews warns us about it. "Make every effort to live in peace with all men and to be holy; without holiness no one will see the Lord. See to it that no one misses the grace of God and that no bitter root grows up to cause trouble and defile many" (Heb. 12:14–15). Claiming ignorance isn't an option either, for "Each heart knows its own bitterness..." (Prov. 14:10).

Bitterness increases when our thoughts and desires are focused "under the sun" (see Ecc. 1:14). Then we compare our lives with the life of others; we listen to the media and its constant barrage of the things we should have; we compare our gifts and talents with those of others; we compare our successes or failures with others; and we compare our trials and sufferings with others. This is how Satan tried to influence Job. He turned Job's sufferings and supposed thoughts about God's justice as an excuse for his bitterness, "I will not keep silent.... I will complain in the bitterness of my soul" (Job 7:11); but he found out that it grieved God, so Job put his hand over his mouth saying, "Surely I spoke of things I did not understand, things too wonderful for me to know" (Job 42:3).

The third root of envy is malice and spite. "A malicious man disguises himself with his lips, but in his heart he harbors deceit. Though his speech is charming, do not believe him, for seven abominations fill his heart (see Proverbs 6:16–19). His malice may be concealed by deception, but his wickedness will be exposed in the assembly" (Prov. 26:24–26). Peter and Paul emphatically tell believers to "Rid yourselves of all malice and all deceit, hypocrisy, envy, and slander of every kind" (1 Pet. 2:1). For malice and spite "grieve the Holy Spirit of God." Instead, "Be kind and compassionate to one another, forgiving each other, just as in Christ God forgave you" (see Eph. 4:29–32).

A fourth root of envy is self-pity, which has an underlying element of fear, a defense mechanism of anger and includes envy, malice, bitterness, and a lack of contentment. Oswald Chambers said, "No sin is worse than the sin of self-pity, because it obliterates God and puts self-interest upon the throne. It opens our mouths to spit out murmurings and our lives become craving spiritual sponges, there is nothing lovely or generous about them."[9] Self-pity is a deeply rooted evil stronghold, denied by most Christians, but often remains because at first it draws caring people to them and brings special attention. Those relationships may change soon, however, if or when people find out they are being used by the person of self-pity and if they see that a person is unwilling to change or face this unfriendly attitude.

I have had much experience with the stronghold of self-pity. For years, my psychiatrists and counselors treated me for depression, even hospitalizing me for six weeks. However, after reading Tim LaHaye's book, *How to Win over Depression,* I realized my problem was not depression but self-pity. LaHaye says, "When stripped of its false façade of excuse making and self-justification, self-pity stands naked and exposed as a mental attitude sin. Those who would be most hesitant to commit an overt act of sin such as adultery or fornication seem to have no compunction against this mental sin."[10] He also mentions his hesitancy to call self-pity a sin because he was the first person to do so, however, many counselors later agreed. When I faced my depression as self-pity and repented, seeking God's forgiveness, it never came back.

In John chapter 5, Jesus asks a disabled man at the pool of Bethesda, who had lived with self-pity for thirty-eight years, "Do you want to get well?" (verse 5).

"'Sir,' the invalid replied, 'I have no one to help me into the pool when the water is stirred. While I am trying to get in, someone else goes down ahead of me'" (verse 7).

Jesus responds, "'Get up! Pick up your mat and walk' At once the man was cured; he picked up his mat and walked" (John 5:8–9). Sometime later, Jesus found him at the temple and said to him, "See, you are well again. Stop sinning or something worse may happen to you" (verse 14).

Notice the question, "Do you want to get well?" That *is* the clue: do we want to get well? Self-pity affects us mentally, emotionally, physically and spiritually—it's an attitude sin.

I wanted to get well, so I repented of my sin of self-pity, which in turn brought my other attitude sins to the surface as well: envy, bitterness, discontent, anger, malice, and spite. After repenting of each one and turning everything over to God for his forgiveness, he cleansed me of my sin, reworked my garden, and taught me thankfulness. Self-pity sees the negative part of life; one that seems to be without blessings, but thankfulness allows our spirit to recognize God's every blessing, which causes daily praise to him and changes all of life.

Jerry Bridges ties thanksgiving to contentment. "Contentment and thanksgiving strengthen each other.... An ungrateful heart (which all of ours are by nature) must be transformed by the renewal of the mind. This transformation is the work of the Holy Spirit as we fill our minds with the word of God."[11] Yes, transformation happens when we "take captive every thought to make it obedient to Christ" (2 Cor. 10:5).

All of Paul's epistles overflow with thankfulness despite his Roman imprisonment and all the other trials and tribulations he faced, including his "thorn in the flesh" of which he boasted. "For when I am weak, then I am strong" (2 Cor. 12:10). When we look at God's work in Paul's life and in mine, we can see why we need to guard our hearts, our emotions, our minds, our souls, our lips, and our behaviors by looking straight ahead, making level paths for our feet and taking only ways that are firm, for all these show evidence of our life in Christ.

Jesus cares for us immensely, just as he cares for the lily of the field, the bird of the air, the grass that grows, and every hair on our head. "No one ever hated his own body, but he feeds and cares for it, just as Christ does the church—for we are members of his body" (Eph. 5:29–30). Just as we care for our bodies, we need to care for our minds and emotions.

QUESTIONS FOR THOUGHT

1. How does envy or covetousness influence your life?
2. What is the outcome of the seed, the Word of God, received by your mind?
3. Which strongholds are present in your life? Depression, bitterness, discontent, self-pity, malice, spite, or others? Describe how you face and change them.
4. How would you describe your value to Jesus and the care he gives you?
5. What place does thankfulness have in your life?
6. Describe all the blessings you have.

CHAPTER 7

LOVE DOES NOT BOAST, IT IS NOT PROUD

L IKE RUDENESS AND envy, boasting and pride come from an unordered garden and grieve the Holy Spirit. Very seldom does pride exist without boastfulness. Pride is a deadly sin and one that most Christians think is impossible for them. They generally sidestep the issue and/or refuse to examine their life to see if it exists. Pride comes in various forms, can slip in unnoticed, and it will take over. I often find myself praying this prayer as a result: "Search me, O God, and know my heart; test me and know my anxious thoughts. See if there is any offensive way in me, and lead me in the way everlasting" (Ps. 139:23–24). "You perceive my thoughts from afar…. Before a word is on my tongue you know it completely, O LORD" (Ps. 139:2–4).

In order to detect pride or boasting, we need to examine our hearts under the microscope of Christ's righteousness, *not* in comparison to other Christians or the world. It is dangerous to believe that pride and boasting isn't or couldn't be part of a Christian's life, because that belief is prideful and separates us from God's purpose or plan. Pride and boasting appear because we have a deep personal need for significance and approval from others. We don't like to be emotionally, mentally, or physically dependent on anyone, including God. From the time we are born, we are defiant of God. However, God requires relationship. He has placed us here to rely on and work with him and each other to show his glory and honor. Therefore, we must battle against pride.

R. C. Sproul explains our deep need for significance. He points out that the desire for importance isn't sinful or evil. If our pursuit is based solely on an inner attitude according to God's will and a willingness to obey his plan, we will end up praising him and bringing him the glory. Submission to God shows we believe we are of significance to him and that he chose us before the foundation of the world—according to his plan, purpose, and will—to save us and then work through us to glorify him (see Eph. 1:11–13). Even though we were chosen according to his plan, Sproul says, "This basic need is difficult to acknowledge and refine:

> We yearn to believe that in some way we are important. This inner drive is as intense as our need for water and oxygen.... The hollow point aches for satisfaction. We dream, we hope, we fantasize our moment in the sun, hoarding the scraps of success in the trophy room of our souls.... I seek to be respected by other people. Those other people also want to be respected.... What happens when our goals collide determines how we value people.... If our climb is over the dead and mutilated bodies of other people, then the aspiration for significance has run amuck.... Self-esteem corrupts to *pride*; the quest for material welfare crosses the border to *covetousness*; the hunger for personal intimacy degenerates to *lust*. Pain turns to *anger* and hunger to *gluttony*. Admiration and honor are sullied by *envy*, and our need for rest surrenders to *sloth*.[1]

Notice the corruption: pride, covetousness, envy, lust, anger, gluttony, sloth, lack of respect, and faulty goals. These are similar to the roots of envy: discontent, bitterness, anger, self-pity, malice, and spite. Les Carter makes note of that when he speaks about how exaggerated pride sets off other emotions. He mentions anger, disillusionment, defeat, depression, anxiety, and guilt. "In every case there is an undue concern for self."[2] Pride and boasting embody many other sinful emotions and behavior. This happens because we forget to seek Christ when we pursue significance and instead we compare our attitude with other Christians, depending on them to fill this significant spot in our lives, yet that is impossible because they, too, are weak and sinful.

Also notice how often anger is part of the equation of faulty emotions and attitudes; our selfish nature wants us to be in control. We are unable to bear second place, failure, or loss of any kind. Anger gives us the energy to keep striving, but it also is the emotion that corrodes our thinking and actions. It either provides the energy to keep fulfilling our goal or it does the reverse and we submit to depression, self-pity, and sloth before finally just giving up. Yet even these later emotions are in a sense a form of pride and boasting for they draw attention from others, only in a negative way.

Another danger that surfaces in our extreme need for significance is criticism, which is either destructive or may be constructive. Destructive criticism carries the thought and action, whether intentional or unintentional, that in belittling or correcting others, our weaknesses, self-esteem, or intelligence will be enhanced. That's not true. After this type of behavior is used against someone, generally guilt and shame enter instead, unless we have a heart that is already hardened and we think so highly of ourselves we don't recognize the difference. The ability to offer constructive criticism comes only from a humble, kind person who is content in the Holy Spirit, and who knows that in Christ is significance (see 1 Tim. 6:11).

Before Paul came to Christ, his attitude carried most of these negative love principles. Christ, however, turned Paul's pursuit of significance to him and now Paul is considered by most to be our greatest apostle. He calls himself the least of the apostles and says that he did not even deserve to be called one for he had persecuted the church (see 1 Cor. 15:9). Further evidence of Paul's tendency to pride is the thorn in the flesh ("a messenger from Satan to torment him") given to him by God to prevent conceit from his special revelations from Christ (see 2 Cor. 12:7). If Paul received a thorn to keep him from pride, we can be sure that our refusal to admit a proneness to pride will bring consequences, if not here, then in heaven. "For by your words you will be acquitted, and by your words you will be condemned" (Matt. 12:37). Our words reflect our inner character.

Another person in Scripture who struggled with pride is King Nebuchadnezzar. He suffered the consequences here on earth. Many times he observed God's power and even made a decree, "that the people of any nation or language who say anything against the God of these men (Daniel and his three friends) would be destroyed" (see Dan. 3:28–30). Yet, these events weren't enough to alter his personal arrogance, boasting, and self-superiority. It took seven years of personal humiliation to finally change him:

> As the king was walking on the roof of the royal palace of Babylon, he said, "Is not this the great Babylon I have built as the royal residence, by my mighty power and for the glory of my majesty?"
>
> The words were still on his lips when a voice came from heaven, "This is what is decreed for you, King Nebuchadnezzar: Your royal authority has been taken from you. You will be driven away from people and will live with the wild animals; you will eat grass like cattle. Seven times will pass by for you until you acknowledge that the Most High is sovereign over the kingdoms of men and gives them to anyone he wishes…."
>
> At the end of that time, I, Nebuchadnezzar, raised my eyes toward heaven, and my sanity was restored. Then I praised the Most High; I honored and glorified him who lives forever. His dominion is an eternal dominion; his kingdom endures from generation to generation…because everything he does is right and all his ways are just. And those who walk in pride he is able to humble.
>
> (Dan. 4:31–37)

King Saul is a third example of a reckless pursuit for significance, and he suffered consequences here on earth and heaven. As a young man, he was impressive physically, "without equal among the Israelites—a head taller than any of the others" (1 Sam. 9:2), humble (1 Sam. 10:21), shy (1 Sam. 10:22), and obedient to his father (1 Sam. 9:5). Saul was anointed by God to be king of Israel to please the people and fulfill their wishes for a king, so God changed Saul's heart (1 Sam. 10:9). King Saul was given great power by God to subdue the enemies of Israel. Unfortunately, all this power turned his head and he became puffed up with pride and finally disobeyed God, whereby he lost his kingship (1 Sam. 13:13–14) and God's love (2 Sam. 7:15).

Both kings suffered humiliation and punishment from God, yet they responded differently. King Nebuchadnezzar repented with praise, glory, and thankfulness to God, but Saul remained disobedient under his masks and excuses and ended up taking his own life (see 1 Sam 31:4–6).

In the New Testament, Jesus unmasked the Pharisees' pride and boasting many times. One example to prove their self-righteousness is when the Pharisees came to trap Jesus by bringing him a woman they said had been caught in adultery. Jesus rebuked them by saying, "If any one of you is without sin, let him be the first to throw a stone at her." All the Pharisees turned away one by one, as Jesus revealed their sin while writing on the ground (see John 8:3–8).

Jesus rebuked the arrogance of his twelve disciples and other followers as well by telling them that anyone who hears his words will practice them, but those who hear and decide not to practice them are "like a man who built a house on the ground without foundation. The moment the torrent struck that house, it collapsed and its destruction was complete" (Luke 6:49). Paul gave many warnings in his epistles for us too, reminding us that a person who is in step with the Spirit doesn't become conceited (see Gal. 5:25–26).

These biblical examples, along with R. C. Sproul's description, show how deeply we crave significance. Because of our sinful nature, we are all going to experience attacks of pride and boasting, but we disobey when we refuse to admit to our sin of pride and repent. As Christians, an unwillingness to face this sin prevents maturity, sanctification, kindness, goodness, and patience—all of which are foundations of love. We are walking in a double-bind lifestyle— saying one thing and doing another, as well as a double-minded one—thinking we may honor God and evil at the same time.

"God uses many ways to teach us dependency on Jesus Christ," said Larry Christianson. "Deep within us, beneath the level that can be reached by our conscious will, exist little pockets of independence which insist that we can live out this or that aspect of our lives on our own.... In order to do this, the Holy Spirit brings into action a very special tool called Trouble. This is a tool... designed to fulfill a twofold function: it has a *cutting edge* and an *etching point*. The cutting edge of trouble exposes our weakness. The etching point inscribes upon the picture of God's strength. Trouble exposes our weakness so that we can learn to draw upon God's strength."[3]

The *cutting edge* and *etching point* of Jesus is this, "You hypocrite, first take the plank out of your own eye, and then you will see clearly to remove the speck from your brother's eye" (Matt. 7:5). Only if and when we learn to be content like Paul, and as "a servant" like Jesus, who, even though he was "equal with God" never boasted about or used his status in a prideful way, will we put on Christ's attitude and "in humility consider others better" than ourselves and look "to the interests of others" (Phil. 2:3–7).

Another *cutting edge and etching point* tool I found helpful was the list of strengths and weaknesses in the book *Spirit Controlled Temperament* by Tim LaHaye.[4] He used four temperaments, traits or personalities noting that one trait or temperament is generally more predominant, but others are also evident. This is not a new technique; other authors have used it with the same or different terms. Discovering our strengths and weaknesses (we do have both) gives us an awareness of the whole facet of our personality. We may not like what we see, but it is worthwhile. The best use of LaHaye's material is to evaluate self, not others. I'm sharing a few of my strengths and weaknesses and how they have affected my relationships.

My primary trait is a Melancholy. My strengths are: sensitive, creative thinking, analytical and detailed, a faithful friend, self-sacrificing, and dependable. My weaknesses: a perfectionist, self-centered, pessimistic, moody-self-contemplation and examination—this can be harmful, and critical—"often conveyed through a proud, haughty and sometimes arrogant attitude." However, "Melancholy people should take great consolation in the fact that many of the most outstanding men in the Bible were predominantly Melancholy. The success, however, of these men was that they 'believe God.' ...The primary needs of the Melancholy are love, joy, peace, goodness, faith, and self-control."

Place Ministries[5] used these same traits that describe an individual's personality to show how they affect relationships. According to Place Ministries, Melancholys "have significant problems in relating. They do not make many friends, but those they make, they keep by being faithful, loyal, and dependable.... However, Melancholy's are hard to get along with or touch, and they are proud. Their sharp ability to analyze lets them see faults in others clearly, and they become critical and judgmental. The Melancholys self-centeredness focuses them on how things affect them, not how they affect others. So they cannot analyze their own faults.... They may be the most likely Personality to create disharmony, blame, whine, and complain."

My second trait is a Choleric. My strengths are: practical-organized, strong willpower, leader, decisive, self-confidence-optimistic, self-disciplined, and intuitive. My weaknesses: hot-tempered-revengeful, cruel, impetuous, aggressive, self-sufficient, angry, proud, and lack compassion. La Haye says, "Of all the temperaments, [a Choleric] probably has the greatest number of spiritual needs, which are love, peace, gentleness, long suffering, meekness and goodness." According to Place Ministries, Cholerics "consider apologizing as perhaps the ultimate humiliation; thus, committing to apologizing consistently can help conquer their relational weaknesses."

As you can see, a Melancholy and Choleric personality has difficulties with relationships and carries a proud and haughty spirit. It's no wonder we need to learn love and have a deep commitment of rest and trust in Christ's redeeming, forgiving mercy. That trust brings the joy and peace we really need and balances our overwhelming need for significance and praise from others. Christ knows and understands the difficulties of these personalities and the Holy Spirit has the power to refine them so that they bear his fruit.

In our search for significance, its measure is found not by comparison with other people, but in Christ. "*If* you have any encouragement from being *united* with Christ, *if* any comfort from his love, *if* any fellowship with the Spirit, *if* any tenderness and compassion, *then*.... Do *nothing* out of selfish ambition or vain conceit,...that at the name of Jesus every knee should bow...and every tongue confess that Jesus Christ is Lord, to the glory of God the Father" (Phil. 2:1–3, 10–11 emphasis mine).

Significance, dignity and humility, according to Andrew Murray are, "the sinner dwelling in the full light of God's holy, redeeming love—in the experience of that full indwelling of divine love, which comes through Christ and the Holy Spirit—who cannot be anything but humble. Not to be occupied with your sin, but to be occupied with God, brings deliverance from self."[6] We find rest for our souls and significance, dignity and humility, when we learn from his teachings in the Sermon on the Mount. They are listed in order of growth and are required by all citizens who wish to enter the kingdom of God.

1. Humility, for the poor in Spirit
2. Comfort, for those who mourn over their sin
3. Gentleness and a patience, followed by meekness
4. Righteousness, when filling our life-long hunger
5. Compassion, when mercy is in action
6. Purity
7. Peacemaker, when we center on the gospel
8. Persecution, or we may need to rethink our Christian life
9. Salt—a purifier—and preservative
10. Light, which shines and doesn't hide

Therefore, "Live in harmony with one another; be sympathetic, love as brothers, be compassionate and humble. Do not repay evil with evil or insult with insult, but with blessing, because to this you were called, so that you may inherit a blessing. For, 'Whoever would love life and see good days must keep his tongue from evil and his lips from deceitful speech. He must turn from evil and do good; he must seek peace and pursue it. For the eyes of the Lord are on the righteous and his ears are attentive to their prayer, but the face of the Lord is against those who do evil'" (1 Pet. 3:8–12).

QUESTIONS FOR THOUGHT

1. How often do you examine yourself to see if pride exists in your heart, and what do you do if you find it?

2. How can understanding the strengths and weaknesses of your personality type make you more aware of what you need to change?

3. How often do you measure your behavior against that of others rather than Scripture?

4. How would you describe your pursuit of humbleness?

5. After you've searched for significance and dignity, how does it compare to humbleness?

6. As a citizen of the kingdom of heaven, how is your growth in comparison with the Sermon on the Mount?

CHAPTER 8

LOVE IS NOT
SELF-SEEKING

WHEN LOVE IS self-seeking it can become manipulative and can carry characteristics similar to rudeness, envy, boastfulness, and pride, so the material covered in those chapters may apply here, also. *Vine's Greek Dictionary* uses the term "self-will" instead of "self-seeking," defining it as behavior that is "self-pleasing, dominated by self-interest and inconsiderate of others arrogantly asserts his/[her] own will."[1] *The Bible Encyclopaedia* adds that it is "a false pride" especially when an individual opposes the "dictates of wisdom or propriety or the wishes of others."[2]

Rick Warren points out that self-seeking behavior may become manipulative. He says that even our service for God may be used as a bargaining tool. "We serve to get others to like us, to be admired, or to achieve our own goals…. The quality of self-forgetfulness, like faithfulness, is extremely rare. Out of all the people Paul knew, Timothy was the only example [of a servant] he could point to. Thinking like a servant is difficult because it challenges the basic problem of my life: I am, by nature, selfish. I think most about me. That's why humility is a daily struggle, a lesson I must relearn over and over."[3]

All Christians will manifest self-seeking attitudes and behavior, but the degree with which they are manifested depends on whether we truly desire to throw off those kinds of attitudes and behavior and instead seek to practice self-control (a fruit of the Spirit). It will also depend on how that selfishness is measured. If it's measured according to the opinions of others, usually no change will occur. However, if God is truly sought, the Holy Spirit *will* work change. However, change *only* occurs when and if we obey his commandments—our responsibility of his work in us.

An example from my life that reflects self-seeking tendencies was my yearning to become a vocalist. I knew I didn't have the natural ability in music like my father, sisters and brothers. Yet, it seemed one way I could find a special place in the Christian community. I had convinced myself it was my way to proclaim God's praise. This was true, but unfortunately, my selfish desires overshadowed honoring God. I received much encouragement from others, for which I am grateful. However, unbeknownst to them, it tended to support my human goal. It was later, when I saw the truth and consciously placed myself under the control of the Holy Spirit that I found contentment in my solo work.

Paul says, "We do not dare to classify or compare ourselves with some who commend themselves. When they measure themselves by themselves and compare themselves with themselves, they are not wise" (2 Cor. 10:12). Instead, as Jesus said, "The Spirit of truth…will guide you into all truth…. He will bring glory to me by taking from what is mine and making it known to you" (John 16:13–14). We see in these verses our lack of wisdom when we pursue a life of self-pleasure, for we are avoiding the truth and the conviction of God's Holy Word.

The more willing we are to drag our selfish, self-seeking desires into the open, the more blessings we receive from the power of the Holy Spirit as we are shaped into the image of Christ. Refusing to face these selfish desires brings complacency and the unawareness of the influence of Satan who wants us content in our old nature—a nature that separates us from the Holy Spirit. Beware, do not make a willful choice to refuse to face selfishness and ignore the lies of Satan. He masquerades as an angel of light and uses his demons as servants of righteousness (see 2 Cor. 11:14). They prowl around like roaring lions trying to devour us (see 1 Pet. 5:8).

King Solomon's life shows Satan's masquerading techniques and influence, despite the great promises God granted him when he asked for a discerning heart to govern God's people and to distinguish between right and wrong (see 1 Kings 3:9). God not only granted that particular promise, but he also gave him wisdom unlike any before or after him (except Christ), riches and honor beyond any other kings, and a long life (see 1 Kings 3:10–14; 4:29). God also promised a royal throne over Israel forever, *if* Solomon walked with integrity of heart and uprightness observing God's commands, decrees, and laws as King David, his father, had done (see 1 Kings 9:4–5).

Unfortunately, King Solomon neglected to remember *all* God's great gifts and answers to his prayers. His father, King David, upon his deathbed gave him a charge to remain strong and a man of God who walks in God's ways, keeping God's requirements so that he would prosper and so that God could keep his own promise to David (see 1 Kings 2:1–4). Solomon forgot his father's charge also and allowed the sinful ways of his childhood home to influence him instead of King David's reverence for God. King Solomon's self-seeking desires led him astray when he took seven hundred wives and three hundred concubines—foreign women from other nations—all of which was forbidden by God. He followed other gods through these wives and God became angry with him, for he turned away from the LORD by doing evil and did not follow the LORD completely (see 1 Kings 11:1–6).

God allows us to make choices, but our choices either reap rewards or they suffer consequences, depending on whether we obey or disobey God. King Solomon made many foolish choices in his life. Besides all his wives and concubines he acquired horses (see 1 Kings 10:26), which God had forbidden (see Deut. 17:16). God punished Solomon with the rod of men, but not with the extreme punishment he gave King Saul, in that God didn't take his love away from King Solomon (see 2 Sam. 7:14–15). However, God took away eleven of the tribes of Israel under his rule and left only Judah to honor his promise to King David—one of David's sons must sit on the throne forever. Sadly, Solomon lost that honor; it went to his brother Nathan (see 1 Chron. 3:5; Luke 3:31; Zach. 12:12).

According to *The Bible Encyclopaedia*, "It is of course true that Solomon often sought self-glorification rather than the glory of God…yet his heart was always in tune with all that would magnify Jehovah…. With all his wisdom, he gave himself up to the pursuit of luxury and splendor for his own sake, forgot the best interests of his people and nearly wrecked his government…. He died as he lived, self-centered."[4] I believe Solomon's writings in his Book of Ecclesiastes show us the battle he waged in his spirit. He searched everything *under the sun* and found it *meaningless*, but his final conclusion was in honor of God. "Fear God and keep his commandments, for this is the whole duty of man. For God will bring every deed into judgment, including every hidden thing, whether it is good or evil" (Ecc. 12:13–14).

David Seamands found from his hours and hours of counseling adults that, "The home is like a skylight through which we glimpse our first pictures of God. We get our earliest "feltness" of God through relating with our parents. A great many of their characteristics are woven into our idea of His character, from what is *caught* as well as *taught*. Few parents realize that whatever is *permitted* in the home is both taught and caught…. The home is like a *window* through which we look at others."[5] King David's sin of adultery and his home permissiveness was *caught* and *taught* by his children. David's punishment from God was a "sword that never departed from his house." This sword was seen in Solomon's life and in the life of his sons Absalom and Amnon (see 2 Sam. 13, 15).

My self-seeking tendencies were *caught* and *taught* in my childhood home—one of rigidity and authoritarian rule. I rebelled, as a child and a teenager, against this type of rule. However, not liking it and knowing how to change rigidity and authoritarianism is two different things. It is my belief that the starvation of true love from this *caught* or *taught* atmosphere comes from parents who haven't learned biblical love either. Dr. Tim Clinton explains how a lack of nurturing along with its ramifications results in emotional or relational injuries, "the source of much pain and madness in the modern world...."

> An early attachment injury results when someone we love, someone who we think should love us, like a parent, fails to provide our fundamental safety and security needs. In the attachment bond, anything that stands in the way of our ability to access our support figure and threatens our sense of security—whether that threat is real or perceived—has the potential to cause an attachment injury. And such injuries can ignite life's core pains: anger, anxiety, fear, grief, and suffering of various kinds.... If the loved one remains unavailable or hurtful...the injury pollutes our soul.[6]

I have come to the conclusion that there's a direct link between attachment injuries and the reading, understanding, and obeying of Scripture. We are commanded to "Train a child in the way he should go, and when he is old he will not turn from it" (Prov. 22:6). We are taught not to anger or frustrate children, but instead to "bring them up in the training and instruction of the Lord" (Eph. 6:4). That means we are to turn them away from self-centeredness and toward the pursuit of righteousness, godliness, faith, love, hope, endurance, gentleness, humbleness, obedience to the truth of God's word and make every effort that leads to peace and to mutual edification.

When a child sustains injuries that pollute the soul, as Dr. Clinton pointed out, he or she will carry that damage into adulthood. We have discussed many of my attachment injuries and this comment by Paul Meier expands on them. "Some research suggests that the parents loving each other is even more important than their love for the youngsters.... Genuine love does not develop without help; it is learned.... Within marriage, genuine love is *emotional*... *physical*...[and] *spiritual*.... This level of mature love, with all three aspects, is found in only a minority of adults; very few people ever reach their true love potential in the marriage relationship."[7] I seldom observed physical or spiritual love between my parents, which they may have kept private. But when I think about their emotional relationship, they seemed to carry an undercurrent of anger toward each other.

Charles Swindoll said unloving attitudes are comparable to a wall of stones, "formidable, intimidating, and thick. They would hold us back from all the things that God intended His people to enjoy." Instead of visible, they are invisible walls of prohibiting grace. "From without: legalism, expectations, traditionalism, manipulation, demands, negativism, control, comparison, perfectionism, competition, criticism, pettiness, and a host of others; and from within: pride, fear, resentment, bitterness, an unforgiving spirit, insecurity, fleshly effort, guilt, shame, gossip, hypocrisy, and many more...grace killers, all!"[8]

So, asks Larry Crabb, "Why is a deep inward look not a natural part of all Christian growth? Why is it avoided and sometimes condemned as self-centeredness? I think the reason is simply fear. We fear the unknown, we fear losing control, we fear spoiling a comfortable existence, we fear facing unpleasant truths about ourselves, and we fear confusion that robs us of certainty in our decisions."[9] Maybe nothing changed in my childhood home either, because of this type of fear: of the unknown, losing control, and facing unpleasant truths, or certainty about decisions.

Notice, all these fears are self-centered. They are battles fought within us between personal wants and pleasures and obeying God. But the man who fears God avoids all extremes (Ecc. 7:18) and has "a reverential fear of God, as a controlling motive of the life, in matters spiritual and moral. Not a mere fear of His power and righteous retribution, but a wholesome dread of displeasing Him, a fear which banishes the terror that shrinks from his presence (Rom. 8:15), and influences the disposition and attitude of one whose circumstances are guided by trust in God, through the indwelling Spirit of God."[10]

In Romans 12, we find the transformational verses for turning around this fearful, self-seeking, performance-based attitude—a transformed mind—from thinking too highly of ourselves to thinking "with sober judgment, in accordance with the measure of faith God has given you." The gift of faith from God through Jesus

Christ measured unto us by the power of the Holy Spirit produces a life of "living sacrifices, holy and pleasing to God."

As David Seamands says, "Any false and immature understanding of the self and self-surrender leaves the person self-sufficient, self-righteous, self-willed, seeking his own glory...unsurrendered.... It is only when I surrender myself to God, when I allow Him to take center stage of my life, when I put myself under His authority, when I am filled with His love, that I can love Him with my whole self. Only then do I possess the true self-esteem and self-love that enables me to love other people. You cannot reverse these two and come out right. Then the true self can be cultivated, accepted, realized, actualized, and developed to its fullest potential."[11]

Paul surrendered his self-seeking, self-righteous life to Christ when he practiced this transformation of his body and mind. "Do you not know that in a race all the runners run, but only one gets the prize? Run in such a way as to get the prize. Everyone who competes in the games goes into strict training.... Therefore I do not run like a man running aimlessly; I do not fight like a man beating the air. No, I beat my body and make it my slave so that after I have preached to others, I myself will not be disqualified for the prize" (1 Cor. 9:24–27).

According to Oswald Chambers, "If you want to know how real you are, test yourself by these words—'Come unto Me.' In every degree in which you are not real, you will dispute rather than come, you will quibble rather than come, you will go through sorrow rather than come, you will do anything rather than come the last lap of unutterable foolishness—'Just as I am.'...You will never get further until you are willing to do that one thing. The Holy Spirit will locate the one impregnable thing in you, but He cannot budge it unless you are willing to let Him."[12]

Jesus taught us how to be self-controlled, reverent, loving, servants, compassionate, and merciful. He took off his outer clothing, wrapped a towel around his waist, and with a basin of water washed his disciples' feet. Then he dried them with his towel. When Jesus was finished, he said, "Now that I, your Lord and Teacher, have washed your feet, you also should wash one another's feet.

I have set you an example that you should do as I have done for you. I tell you the truth, no servant is greater than his master, nor is a messenger greater than the one who sent him. Now that you know these things, you will be blessed if you do them" (John 13:14–17).

QUESTIONS FOR THOUGHT

1. If you searched inside and compared your life with God's truth, what would it look like?

2. What kind of examples and attachments are *caught* and *taught* in your home? When you compare the "feltness" of God the Father, how does that look according to Scripture?

3. If you were being observed, what kind of love would others see? What unloving attitudes of prohibiting grace would be there?

4. Where in your life do you see self-seeking tendencies and how do you measure them, by other people or according to God's word?

5. What act equivalent to the washing of a person's feet have you done lately?

6. Where would your measurement (washing feet) fall in comparison to Christ's mercy and humbleness?

CHAPTER 9

LOVE IS NOT EASILY ANGERED, IT KEEPS NO RECORD OF WRONGS

TOWARD THE END of the last chapter, we noted how Paul compared his surrendered Christian journey to a race by beating his body to make it his slave, so that after he preached to others, he would not be disqualified for the prize. As a legalistic Pharisee and persecutor of the Christians, Paul, not only pursued a lifestyle of self and performance, he also exhibited anger and was well qualified to give this admonition to the Corinthians as well as to us, "Love is not easily angered, it keeps no record of wrongs."

Vine's Greek Dictionary defines anger as "the strongest of all passions,"[1] so if we claim that we love while at the same time we are easily angered and keep a record of wrongs, then we are in sin. In Christ, we are commanded to develop and live the fruit of self-control. Self-control is a manifestation of the gift and power of the Holy Spirit, fully conscious of our sin with the need for repentance, while we make every effort to put on "faith and love as a breastplate, and the hope of salvation as a helmet" (1 Thess. 5:8).

I attest to the fact that anger is the strongest of passions. In the chapter on rudeness, we looked at the lies of perfectionism and a performance-based lifestyle. David Seamands says that he has yet "to counsel a performance-based and perfectionistic Christian who was not at heart *an angry person*" (emphasis Seamands').

They often impress us as being extremely controlled or very loving.... They struggle with resentments and sometimes even rage, and their seemingly uncontrollable outbursts of temper are the major factor in disrupting their personal relationships at work, in church, and especially with their spouses and children. They come across as angry persons and angriest at themselves for being the way they are. This, of course, creates a vicious circle which increases their guilt, low self-esteems, and their sense of being phony....[2]

The main reason for my need to learn how to love was because of my character of anger. As John Bradshaw explains, "The person doesn't have anger or melancholy, she *is* angry and melancholy.... If you were never allowed to express anger in your family, your anger becomes an alienated part of yourself.... There is no way to get rid of your emotional power of anger. Anger is the self-preserving and self-protecting energy. Without this energy you become a doormat and a people-pleaser."[3]

All the individuals of my childhood home, my marriage, and my children dealt with an angry spirit. We all expressed anger—my character was anger. However, we failed to admit and acknowledge that anger. It was simply disregarded. Most people find it hard to recognize or acknowledge anger, so it is generally denied by using other terms such as, I'm frustrated, hurt, annoyed, etc., which are actually other terms for anger. However, anger cannot be hidden because it is the root of all the other negative emotions, and will surface in one way or another either verbally or nonverbally and negatively or positively. I heard a speaker say that anger is the hardest emotion to overcome and retrain.

Glenn Taylor and Rod Wilson point out that anger is a key theme in Scripture and define it as, "an emotion of displeasure, hurt, shame, pain, indignation, resentment, exasperation, or annoyance, all of which may range from mild to extreme. It manifests itself in criticizing, yelling, withdrawing, feelings of helplessness, shame, victimhood, scorn, scolding, ridiculing, humiliating, despising, teasing, putting down, or...hitting, hurting, damaging, [and] attacking." They also describe its two ways of expression: there is imploding bursting inward anger by suppression, repression, or burying it, which seems hidden, yet surfaces through "feelings, actions, or spiritual abuse directed toward one's self." Or there is an exploding burst of outward anger, directed toward others, things, or God by "venting the emotions with temper or aggression."[4]

My anger generally burst outward, but it was inward when I directed anger toward myself. If anything went wrong, I generally blamed others first, then I turned around and accepted fault so that I kept the person's approval. The problem was that after I left a situation where my anger was displayed outwardly or inwardly, that wasn't the end of the problem. I usually continued the anger process trying to resolve the issue in my mind and convince myself that it was the other person's fault, which at times it may have been.

Taylor and Wilson say that many behaviors can be mechanisms to distort the real emotion of anger. "Masks may be used with intentionality or with a lack of consciousness. They frequently will have deep-seated roots in one's family of origin where they may have been learned. The person's personal or corporate safety may be sought through masking, or the person may function in this way to protect others from what is perceived by the person to be an uncontrollable and dangerous burst of energy and emotion."[5]

It might be good to note the difference between becoming angry and becoming easily angered. As image bearers of God, we have the emotion of anger, which means we will become angry. But, like James said, we must, "be quick to listen, slow to speak and slow to become angry, for man's anger does not bring about the righteous life that God desires" (James 1:19–21). God's righteous anger is expressed every day (see Ps. 7:11), lasts only a moment (see Ps. 30:5), and "is a holy wrath against sin," says *The Bible Dictionary*.[6] His anger is sovereign, perfect, righteous, forgiving, loving, and just.

God may express his righteous anger immediately, as toward Uzzah who touched the ark, an irreverent act (see 2 Sam. 6:6–7). It may come after several warnings, like his dealings with Israel, who were told, repeatedly, that he was their God and they should have no other gods besides him, yet his warnings and calls for repentance weren't heeded (see Ps. 78:8). It may come with a pronouncement of future judgment, like the punishment of King Manasseh's sin (see 2 Kings 21 and 24:3). It may come as justice for sins against others, such as Cain's anger against his brother, Abel, whom he murdered because God had looked favorably on Abel's sacrifice and not Cain's. Or it may come against the willful disobedience of Jonah's self-righteous anger, because he anticipated God's acts before they happened and didn't like it. Everyone who witnessed and we who read about God's acts of righteous anger learn an important lesson about his holiness and justice.

Let's look at King David's response to the death of Uzzah. His anger actually covered another emotion—fear "he was afraid of the LORD that day" (2 Sam. 6:9). Again, we encounter fear as an obstruction to healthy emotions and attitudes. Les Carter says that our display of anger is often *the emotional response that is tied to one's psychological sense of self-preservation.... While anger was meant to have a positive function, we tend to misuse it most of the time.... Most angry people would agree that there are usually two sides to any argument. Yet because of personal insecurities or chronic mistrust of others, angry people usually exhibit an unwillingness to survey all sides of an issue until their needs are satisfactorily resolved.*"[7]

The Bible has a lot to say about anger: "Do not make friends with a hot-tempered man, do not associate with one easily angered, or you may learn his ways and get yourself ensnared" (Prov. 22:24–25). "As churning the milk produces butter, and as twisting the nose produces blood, so, stirring up anger produces strife" (Prov. 30:33). God hates "a man who stirs up dissension among brothers" (Prov. 6:19). Whenever we let the sun go down on our anger, we give the devil a foothold, so we must get rid of all anger, brawling, slander, malice (see Eph. 4:26–31) and the evil that is so prevalent.

We will probably neglect overcoming our sinful anger unless we understand the factors that contribute to it. Glenn Taylor and Rod Wilson mentioned that it is frequently a "deep-seated root in one's family of origin!" That's where mine originated. Charles Swindoll explained in the last chapter about "invisible walls of prohibiting grace," that is certainly true about anger, both in receiving grace and giving grace. A person of anger eventually hides because they do not trust anyone, as John Townsend explains,

> A part of our character is pushed away from relationship into a spiritual darkness called isolation. The isolation of some part of our soul from love.... Yet Jesus Himself stressed the necessity of relationship in order to take in truth.... The entire first year of life is ideally built around helping the infant to take in, or internalize, this sense of belonging and safety.... Emotional object constancy...a state of feeling connected even when one is alone or 'being rooted and grounded in love' (Eph. 3:17 NASV).[8]

How ironic and sad. We yearn for relationships, yet we hide from close relationships, which leads to this type of isolation and enhances our loneliness—loneliness not only when alone, but also in a crowd. We then dread isolation, but the fear of establishing relationships is so much greater that we choose to remain in isolation and loneliness. Connecting is probably the hardest work I do every day, but now that I've faced my anger, my isolation problems, and my fears, I no longer run away. I keep facing all these fears daily, choosing to establish better relationships and learn to practice kindness and patience, foregoing the need to stay where it is safe.

Another contributing factor to anger from the family of origin is anxiety. Les Carter says constant anxiety, fretting or worry "is often a mixture of fear and anger. That is, in worry there is both a feeling of timidity and a sense of irritation."[9] Think of King David, who was both angry and afraid of God! Archibald Hart adds that a child learns anxiety from parents, friends, or "they may discover it for themselves. But once the pattern of constant worry begins, it can become a millstone around a child's neck."[10]

Scripture, however, tells us not to worry about our life (see Matt. 6:25, 27, 34) and to "not be anxious about anything, but in everything, by prayer and petition, with thanksgiving, present your requests to God" (Phil. 4:6). In order to put this Scriptural truth to work, it is not effective to just offer clichés. The only way to change an anxious heart and mind is to seek the Holy Spirit to find the origin of the anxieties, then pray through the problem to eradicate the behavior and replace it with the truth.

Frank Minirth, Paul Meier, and Don Hawkins "believe that a person becomes anxious when he is afraid to look at a negative emotion inside of him. The emotion could be anger, guilt, lust, envy, greed, resentment or some other less-than-positive motive. Rather than face the emotion, he buries it, denies it, ignores it, and refuses to let it surface and be seen. God knows better. In His infinite wisdom, He wants each of us to examine our emotions. To deny our true feelings is to deceive ourselves. Deceit is wrong; it's a lie. The Holy Spirit uses anxiety to tug at our attention and to tell us that something needs to be aired. Anxiety becomes similar to a smoke signal that alerts us to a problem smoldering under the surface."[11]

How true it is that the Holy Spirit brings our anxieties to the surface. One way this happens is through physical problems. Glenn Taylor and Rob Wilson point out that long periods of stressful anger from the physiological arousal of the autonomic nervous system "may lead to…the onset of psychosomatic symptoms." I've included a few symptoms from Taylor and Wilson's list that might indicate anger problems: "gastrointestinal complaints, stomach sensitivity, ulcers, colitis, low-grade infections, a variety of headaches including migraine, hypertension, and viral-like symptoms: fatigue, chronic exhaustion and muscle or joint pain."[12]

After King David committed adultery with Bathsheba and murdered her husband Uriah, we see that psychosomatic problems affected his relationships and his physical, mental and spiritual state (see Psalms 32, 38, and 51). His bones wasted away, his strength was sapped, his back was filled with searing pain, his heart pounded, his strength was gone, and the light vanished from his eyes. His ears and mouth were affected and his friends stayed far from him. In Psalm 51, David repented and it brought healing and transformation to his body, mind, and soul.

According to Larry Crabb, "In every instance, the wrong negative emotion can be traced to a wrong assumption about how personal needs can be met.... I will evaluate whatever happens to me in such a way that I will not feel depression, crippling guilt, resentment, frustration [anger], or anxiety.... Anxiety, resentment [anger], and guilt are the basic problem conditions behind all other personal difficulties."[13] When we think or operate according to our personal wants and desires using negative emotions of anger and anxiety to rule us, we build deadly strongholds.

Recovery from the sin of anger and keeping a record of wrongs only comes when we readily admit it, heed the instruction of Paul—to face our anger before the sun goes down so the devil doesn't build a stronghold—repent, accept the LORD's forgiveness and then do what Les Carter suggests. We must develop "self-confidence to withstand life's imperfections.... Although anger cannot be shut off instantly like a water faucet, it is possible to gain enough control over anger to determine the degree and direction of it. Anger is a choice; it does not have to be a dominant emotion in our lives."[14]

Only God can give us self-confidence (see Prov. 3:26; 1 John 5:14; Heb. 13:6), and it is built or developed when we trust in his wisdom—wisdom that *believes* and doesn't *doubt,* when and if we ask God for that wisdom. He promised, if we ask not doubting, he would give his wisdom generously to all without finding fault. A doubting person is double-minded and unstable in everything, says James (see James 1:5–8). We find great wisdom, self-confidence and the correct perspective about anger "to withstand life's imperfections" through prayer and the prayerful study of the Word of God through the power of the Holy Spirit.

> "You have heard that it was said to the people long ago, 'Do not murder.... I tell you that anyone who is angry with his brother will be subject to judgment.'... Therefore, if you are offering your gift at the altar and there remember that your brother has something against you, leave your gift there in front of the altar. First go and be reconciled to your brother; then come and offer your gift."
>
> (Matt. 5:21–24)

As Paul said, we will not have our attitudes and characteristics perfectly changed "until the day of Christ" (Phil. 1:6), but the confidence and joy we find as we cultivate our inner garden, relearn, and practice new behaviors (deal with all anger before the sun goes down) is beyond explanation. It is possible to change an angry character: we do not allow ourselves to grow bitter, we do not go to bed at night and rationalize a situation until we convince ourselves we displayed righteous anger, we deal with anger honestly, we acknowledge it, we repent from it, accept God's forgiveness, and most importantly, we forgive ourselves. The more we repeat this process, slowly our character changes.

Honesty is an important factor in dealing with our old behaviors. We seldom apply new ones if we don't have a sincere desire to be rid of the old. Robert Harvey and David Benner assure us that, "Honesty comes when the forgiver takes the strides in reinterpreting hurt that introduces new truth into the situation. Up until then our damaged emotions tend to distort how we perceive both the one who hurt us and ourselves. In our woundedness, our perceptions are shaped by our feelings. For healing to occur, our perceptions must be brought into line with reality, with truth. The essence of this reinterpretation of my hurt is seeing those who hurt me as separate from what they did to me and seeing myself as more than my wound."[15]

Honesty, with conviction, came to me from many things: the Bible, books, counseling, speakers, and personal experiences. Instead of comparing myself to others, I first had to put into practice Harvey and Brenner's words in the above paragraph. I had to focus on the preaching of the Word, not the people, place the discipleship of love from the church in God's hands realizing that, I, too, might be distorting the truth and practice my repeated prayer, "Trust in the LORD with all my heart and lean not on my own understanding; but in all my ways acknowledge him, so he will make my paths straight" (a personalized version of Prov. 3:5–6).

Our confidence and wisdom increases when we have the correct understanding of God's enduring, forgiving love. Here, too, love and forgiveness cannot be separated. It's because God forgave the sin of Adam and Eve that he promised the gift of his Son. His forgiveness and love act simultaneously in redemption and we need to act accordingly. Paul tells us to, "Bear with each other and forgive whatever grievances we may have against one another. Forgive as the Lord forgave you" (Col. 3:13). Recovery from anger is centered on forgiveness and bound together in love, then, all reach perfect unity.

I like the way Robert Harvey and David Benner explain forgiveness. I've listed only the main topics from their book where they explain in depth the biblical authors' portrayal of "the blessing of receiving God's forgiving grace." Forgiveness produces: "a sense of cleanness, a sense of guilt decisively removed, a sense of healing and emotional release, a new clarity of mind about God's purpose, and a new unity between persons. Whereas the absence of forgiveness produces: a clinging sense of uncleanness and lostness, a sense of unresolved guilt, a continuing sense of woundedness and longing for healing, darkness of mind and confusion about God's purpose, and a growing disunity between persons even within the Christian fellowship."[16]

When we speak about forgiveness and love, it's important to clarify the oft-repeated phrase, "just forgive and forget." That is impossible and based on an untruth. We are not programmed to forget, but we must trust in the power of the Holy Spirit and his ability to help us keep forgiving and not hold the offense against another. David Stoop and James Masteller say, "The power lies in the fact that we forgive *even as we remember*. If we really forgot, we could not forgive. How could we forgive an offense we are not even aware of? The power of forgiveness is that, even in the face of inescapable reality, it liberates us from the inner anger, the resentment, the quest for vengeance that eats away at us and, in the end, destroys us."[17]

It is my belief that when God ordained his new covenant with the Israelites and promised them that he would remember their sins no more (see Jer. 31:34; 50:20), and repeated that promise to us in Hebrews 10:17, he didn't mean he completely forgot those sins. Because God also said, "He will expose the motives of men's hearts..." (1 Cor. 4:5); he will judge every careless word... spoken (Matt. 12:36); and every deed...whether it is good or evil (Ecc. 12:14). This is not a contradiction. This means that God no longer holds these *forgiven* sins against us now, nor in eternity, because once each sin is repented of and forgiven, they remain forgiven; Jesus took them to the cross. We must simply believe and trust his promised word and his unfailing forgiveness.

Sincere honesty, without doubt in God's wisdom, then, is the foundation of our confession, repentance, forgiveness, and love. In Christ, we crucify the sinful nature with its passions and desires (see Gal. 5:24). Then, in humility, we are able to accept the word planted in us, which can save us (see James 1:21). When we gain wisdom and stay firm in our belief and trust in God, our transformation is completed through the power of the Holy Spirit. Our steadfast confidence in God gives us the humility and ability to love others with forgiveness. All these foundations protect us from the sin of anger.

QUESTIONS FOR THOUGHT

1. What place does anger have in your life? How willing are you to resolve your anger before the sun goes down so the devil doesn't get a foothold?

2. What place does harboring hate or murder have in your heart toward your neighbor?

3. How willing are you to resolve differences, personally, without discussing them with others?

4. How willing are you to crucify the sinful nature with its passions and desires?

5. How often do you hold grudges or keep a record of wrongs?

6. What grudge are you presently carrying?

7. How important is the application of "forgiveness with grace" and "honesty with conviction" for your life, as well as to others?

CHAPTER 10

LOVE DOES NOT DELIGHT IN EVIL, BUT REJOICES WITH THE TRUTH

WHEN WE REJOICE with the truth, rather than delighting in evil, we put to death rudeness, envy, pride, boasting, self-seeking, anger that comes easily, and keeping a record of wrongs—all of which are evidences of our sinful nature. We don't lie to each other either, since we have taken off our old self with its practices and have put on the new self. Instead, the Word of Christ dwells in us richly as we teach and admonish one another with all wisdom.

LOVE DOES NOT DELIGHT IN EVIL

If God is love, why does He allow evil? *The Bible Dictionary* informs us that, "the Scriptures indicate that evil has been permitted by God in order that His justice might be manifested in its punishment and His grace in its forgiveness." As the potter, God has the right to make out of the same lump of clay some pottery for noble purposes and some for common use. He has the right to show mercy, compassion, and harden whom he wills, so that his power is proclaimed in all the earth (see Rom. 9:15–21). We see this in the life of Job when God allowed Satan to test Job with extreme suffering and where

God proved his control over evil, as well as his sovereign justice and protection of Job's life and integrity.

Job was thoroughly confused as to why he suffered such a trial and questioned God's justice, because he couldn't find anything in his life that might have led to his physical and emotional loss. What I find comforting is that God *did* respond to Job, not in the way Job was expecting, but with the awesomeness of his sovereignty. After God admonished him, Job humbly replied, "Surely I spoke of things I did not understand, things too wonderful for me to know" (Job 42:3). Job learned, as we must, that God's thoughts are not our thoughts, neither are his ways our ways. As the heavens are higher than the earth, so are God's ways higher than our ways and God's thoughts than our thoughts (Isa. 55:8–9).

Paul exhorted the Corinthian church because they delighted in evil rather than rejoicing with the truth of the gospel. They followed false teachers and false teachings. Paul warned them, "Do not be misled: 'Bad company corrupts good character.' Come back to your senses as you ought, and stop sinning" (1 Cor. 15:33–34). We, also, have a choice—decide like the Corinthian church and follow the lies of Satan, or decide like Job and trust God. We should never be surprised at the presence of evil, but we should be stunned, amazed, and deeply thankful for God's undeserved forgiveness.

Evil is part of our world, the Bible tells us, and we must always be aware of its great power, influence, and danger (see Eph. 6:10–18). We wander toward evil when we vacillate, lack trust, are drawn into complacency, neglect the Holy Spirit, and refuse to obey the truth. We fit this description by Charles Swindoll, who quotes Wilbur Reese, "I would like to buy $3 worth of God, please, not enough to explode my soul or disturb my sleep, but just enough to equal a cup of warm milk or a snooze in the sunshine. I don't want enough of Him to make me love a black man or pick beets with a migrant. I want ecstasy, not transformation. I want the warmth of the womb, not a new birth. I want a pound of the Eternal in a paper sack. I would like to buy $3 worth of God, please."[1]

God rebuked Israel, and Jesus rebuked the Pharisees with God's very words, because they didn't want transformation either, only

$3 worth of God. The evil in their lives had become their pride of life. "These people honor me with their lips, but their hearts are far from me. They worship me in vain; their teachings are but rules taught by men" (Matt. 15:8–9; see also Isa. 29:13). They were hypocrites. They nullified God's commands for their own selfish purposes and their own manmade laws. We must not get too smug here because we often imitate the Israelites and the Pharisees (see 1 Cor. 10:11).

Andrew Murray said, "Study much to know the written Word; but study more to know the living Word, in whom you are of God. Jesus, the wisdom of God, is only known by a life of implicit confidence and obedience. The words He speaks are spirit and life to those *who live in Him*. Therefore, each time you read, or hear, or meditate upon the Word, be careful to take up your true position. Realize first your oneness with Him who is the wisdom of God; know yourself to be under His direct and special training; go to the Word abiding in Him, the very fountain of divine light—in His light you shall see light."[2]

REJOICING WITH THE TRUTH

J. I. Packer provides three areas to test us *with* the truth: "First… *personal* dealing: Knowing about Him is a necessary precondition of trusting in Him…. But the width of our knowledge about Him is no gauge of the depth of our knowledge of him…. Second… *personal involvement,* in mind, will, and feeling…. 'O taste and see that the Lord is good' said the Psalmist (Ps. 34:8)…. We must not lose sight of the fact that knowing God is an emotional relationship, as well as an intellectual and volitional one…. Third…a matter of *grace.* It is a relationship in which the initiative throughout is with God—*We* do not make friends with *God; God* makes friends with *us,* bringing us to know Him by making His love known to us."[3]

First, *personal* dealing:
The word *with* used in the phrase "rejoicing *with* the truth" has deep importance. It is defined by Webster as, "Having as a possession,

attribute, accoutrement, bearing, wearing, or owning." The Apostle John said, "We know that we have come to know him if we obey his commands. The man who says, 'I know him,' but does not do what he commands is a liar, and the truth is not in him…. This is how we know we are in him: Whoever claims to live in him must walk as Jesus did" (1 John 2:3–6).

We know Satan's temptations will come, yet God is faithful. He will not let us be tempted beyond what we can bear. But when we are tempted, he will also provide a way out so that we can stand up under it (see 1 Cor. 10:13). The way of escape comes through prayer: "Lead us not into temptation, but deliver us from the evil one" (Matt. 6:13) and feasting daily from his words of truth: "I am the bread of life. He who comes to me will never go hungry, and he who believes in me will never be thirsty" (John 6:35). From his Word we taste with our heart the realities to which the Holy Spirit convicts. We find security, encouragement, and sustenance.

Andrew Murray explains how that happens. "*We must live and experience truth in order to know it*…. Receive what you do not comprehend, submit to what you cannot understand, accept and expect what to reason appears a mystery, believe what looks impossible, walk in a way which you know not—such are the first lessons in the school of God. '*If ye abide* in my word, *ye shall understand* the truth.'…The believing surrender to Christ, and the submission to His word, to expect what appears most improbable, is the only way to the full blessedness of knowing Him."[4]

After Jesus explained the power of his *hidden word* to the two men walking to Emmaus and left them, they asked each other, "Were not our hearts burning within us while he talked with us on the road and opened the Scriptures to us?" (Luke 24:32. See also Luke 24:13–35). Does our heart burn when we hear the truth from Scripture? Are we one of Jesus' sheep who listen to his voice and follow him? Does our soul pant and thirst for the living God? Are our days and nights spent in songs and prayers directed by his love? Do we find our hope in him?

According to Jerry Bridges, "Obedience to the will of God…is the ultimate test of our fear of God, and the only true response to

His love for us.... We realize that our sins as Christians, though perhaps not as outwardly gross as before, are more heinous in the sight of God because they are sins against knowledge and against grace. We know better and we know His love, and yet we sin willfully. And then we go back to the cross and realize that Jesus bore even those willful sins in His body on the tree, and the realization of that infinite love compels us to deal with those very sins and to put them to death. Both the fear of God and the love of God motivate us to obedience, and that obedience proves they are authentic in our lives."[5]

Second—*personal involvement* in mind, will, and feeling:
Submitting our entire life means *one* choice—submission to the whole truth. There is no vacillating back and forth. Charles Stanley says there are "three primary areas [God] wants us to compre-hend...*truth about himself...truth about ourselves...* [and] *truth about other people....* Our spiritual mindset in hearing and appropriating scriptural truth greatly affects how we listen to God." If we don't listen to God, we go in the opposite direction. Our minds do not stay in neutral.

> Listening to God and obeying Him are the only constructive methods that enable us to survive the storms of the twentieth century. Hearing His Voice and integrating it into our value systems, behavioral patterns, thoughts, and conversations are the prerequisites for enduring lives. Staying alert and responsive to His speaking Voice becomes the rock foundation that no tempest, temptation, or trial can erode. That's why it's dangerous to attend church, listen to religious broadcasts, or read Christian publications! It's dangerous because Jesus said everyone who hears His truth and does not act upon it will be like the foolish man who built his house upon the sand. It's perilous, because each of us will be held accountable for acting upon every spiritual truth we hear.[6]

Christ said, "Everyone on the side of truth listens to me" (John 18:37). When we listen, our entire being is filled with the fruit of the Spirit and we bear the fruit of Jesus, which is truth. We see this in the biblical story about Daniel and his three friends who were often tempted by the Babylonian king and his astrologers and officers with promises of earthly rewards, high places in the kingdom, and threatened with severe punishments if they didn't forsake God and yield to their requests. Yet, because they stood firm in God, they *never* yielded even when they were threatened with death. God was faithful to their devotion with protection and proved that his will was sovereign.

Our *personal involvement* in mind, will, and feeling will happen when we stand firm like Daniel. The gospel was written so we would believe in Jesus Christ. "Blessed is the man who does not walk in the counsel of the wicked...but his delight is in the law of the LORD.... He is like a tree planted by streams of living water." (Ps. 1:1–3). May we hear the gospel, believe, walk with joy and peace, and rejoice *with* that truth.

Third—a matter of *grace*:
Once we were alienated from God and we were counted among his enemies. But now we are reconciled to Christ through the death of his physical body so we can be presented holy in his sight, without blemish and free from accusation—*if we* continue in our faith, established and firm, not moved from the hope held out in the gospel (see Col. 1:15–23). It's a matter of *grace*!

Beware though, "The gospel offends," say Drs. Dan Allender and Tremper Longman III. "It strikes at the heart of man's arrogance and rage. It demands a response of brokenness—or evokes mockery and contempt. The gospel does not settle for good, moral living; it requires radical transformation of the heart. In that sense, *the calling for every Christian is to prophetically live out a disruptive goodness that embraces foolishness before the wise and weakness before the strong.* To do otherwise—to live merely for another paycheck or summer vacation—is to live for legitimate desires that never attain the dignity and honor of our highest calling."[7]

We are told in Zechariah that the LORD hates evil but loves truth and peace (see Zech. 8:16–19). This statement is preceded with the picture of a garden that is well planted; the seed is sown, the vine yields fruit, and the ground produces. The loving grace of the gospel transforms and cultivates our garden to resemble the first garden in Scripture, the Garden of Eden. Christ continues the picture of a transformed garden in the Gospels when he relates God's Word to seed sown into our hearts through the message of the gospel and to its receptiveness. Our garden has a Gardener, the Father; a Vine, Christ; and the Holy Spirit, the Spirit of Truth, who resides within us and prunes us, the branches, according to Christ's truth.

QUESTIONS FOR THOUGHT

1. What place does evil have in your life?

2. How serious is your battle against a life of complacency and/or straddling two paths?

3. If a $3 value of God were measured in your life, what would you find?

4. How much time do you spend adding to your faith and making your calling and election sure (see 2 Pet. 1:3–10)?

5. What place does rejoicing *with* the truth have in your life?

6. Are you willing to test your eyes, ears, mouth, heart, and soul according to that truth?

7. What would be the test results in your life if you followed J. I. Packer's methods?

CHAPTER 11

LOVE ALWAYS PROTECTS

OSWALD CHAMBERS, ONE of my greatest mentors, says, "If human love does not carry a man beyond himself, it is not love. If love is always discreet, always wise, always sensible and calculating, never carried beyond itself, it is not love at all. It may be affection, it may be warmth of feeling, but it has not the true nature of love in it.... Abandon to God is of more value than personal holiness.... When we are abandoned to God, He works through us all the time.[1]

Chambers describes the concept of Christ "in us"—the place in which Christ's gentle and humble truths transform our inner garden. Once Christ has done so, we can offer protective love to others, as we continue on in the faith.

LOVE ALWAYS PROTECTS

John Townsend said, "Since God created us for bonding, it's part of our very essence, just as it is in His essence. We cannot *not* bond. We are created to bond in either a growth-producing or a death-producing manner. If we cannot bond to loving relationships, we will bond to something else that is not so loving. This is the root of the addictive process. It's also the root of Satan's

101

strategy to sabotage our maturity process.... Many committed Christians are unknowing "sanctified addicts" of otherwise good things that help keep them away from a black hole of loneliness in their hearts and the crucial necessity of close relationships.... The same heart yearns for satisfying and safe human attachments in which we can be truly known and truly loved, that we may all be one."[2]

When we live with the belief that God's boundaries in our submission to him are conditions instead of responsibilities, we create a "death-producing," non-bonding relationship. God's love never changes, but ours does. The disciples went through much training before they became apostles. We need that training, too, in order to extend God's protection to others. The more we view the LORD's boundaries as beneficial training for us, the greater our "growth-producing" and the more we become approved as workmen for his kingdom.

While working with a street ministry in the inner city from 1983 to 1988, I learned the benefits of hugging and interacting with clients who were considered by many as non-huggable. They helped me tear away the prior teaching of stereotyping people and their circumstances. The clients, as we called them, slowly allowed me to become part of their lives as we built relationships. We learned to care for each other through our interactions, and they protected me, while I was their volunteer supervisor, from other clients who might have harmed me inside or outside the building.

Because of my co-dependent personality, I honestly didn't think I had the ability to provide for myself after my divorce in February 1991, after 32 years of marriage. God removed that fear and adequately provided me with steady employment until I retired. (Thankfully, my children were all married.)

It took a few years for me to recognize and understand that God was actually protecting me when he allowed my divorce from a man who only claimed he was a Christian (see 1 Cor. 7:15). That realization, however, did not make my life easier or decrease the sorrow at the loss of my marriage. The problem was, I was caught in a lie because of my weakness for my husband's approval and love. This lie never changed my relationship with my husband; it only drew me away from God. When God calls us to be his disciple and issues a command, he wants a growth-producing relationship, which demands complete obedience (see Luke 14:33; Gen. 22:12). (May I share, before this book went to print, my ex-husband surrendered his life to Christ).

In May 1998, I was diagnosed with a two-centimeter acoustic neuroma—a benign growing fibroid tumor. During the subsequent seven-hour brain surgery, the doctors needed to remove the right hearing and balance nerves while trying to save the facial nerve. Praise the LORD my surgery was a success. My primary surgeon called me "his miracle." I'm positive this miracle came from the folded hands of the many friends, church, family, and co-workers who prayed for me the whole time.

Then, on January 15, 2001, I was spared, physically, with only minor injuries, after a terrible car accident. I missed a stop sign, hit a car broadside and shoved it into a tree killing the driver and injuring the passenger. I was charged with negligent homicide and a medium misdemeanor (lowered from high) and sentenced with a fine and forty hours of unsupervised community service with the non-profit organization for whom I worked. Gratefully, the suffering family didn't seek retribution and the many letters of reference sent to the judge (at the initiative of a church member), helped spare me from a jail sentence, which the judge started to render and then changed his mind in mid-sentence. If it seems as though my sentence was light, it wasn't! Every time I step in the car, the tragedy haunts me, even though I know God has forgiven me.

This book is a testimony of God's protective, unfailing love. I have received further learning, training, assurance, and growth in his Word, which testifies of the powerful guidance of the Holy Spirit. I can attest to the words of Paul. "Think of what you were when you were called. Not many of you were wise by human standards; not many were influential; not many were of noble birth. But God chose the foolish...the weak...the lowly...the despised...and the things that are not—to nullify the things that are, so that no one may boast before him" (1 Cor. 1:26–29).

God proved his faithfulness ever since I was instructed to learn how to love. He sustained me during my divorce, my corrections, rebukes, discipline, and training. He has protected and covered me with his enduring love, patience, kindness, and trustworthiness, and he has provided his confidence, refuge, and fortress, for which I give him praise.

LOVE ALWAYS PROTECTS UNDER GRACE

We mentioned the matter of grace in the last chapter. We also need to understand that our protection is by God's grace, and we in turn are commanded to willingly extend this grace to others, while facing the performance attitudes and behavior of our Christian culture. As a professional counselor, David Seamands assists us in the importance of that understanding:

> I am convinced that the basic cause of some of the most disturbing emotional/spiritual problems which trouble evangelical Christians is the failure to receive and live out God's unconditional grace, and the corresponding failure to offer that grace to others. I encounter this problem in the counseling room more than any other single hangup....
>
> The basic difficulties for performance-minded Christians do not arise from the mind—reason and logic. Merely changing their mental concept of grace will not free them from the bondage of life on the performance grindstone. Grace may begin for them as a doctrinal concept, but it must become an experience which finally saturates their emotions as well. *Grace needs to be fully realized...to penetrate and permeate the heart.... In the Bible heart means every area and function of the personality.*[3]

Dietrich Bonoeffer said that the experience of grace to an obedient, humble, and repentant heart emotionally, spiritually, and mentally is a battle and a choice. He also said that if grace remains merely doctrinal, it soon becomes *cheap grace*. "The grace which amounts to the justification of sin without the justification of the repentant sinner who departs from sin and from whom sin departs. Cheap grace is not the kind of forgiveness of sin, which frees us from the toils of sin. Cheap grace is the grace we bestow on ourselves. Cheap grace is the preaching of forgiveness without repentance, baptism without church discipline, communion without confession, absolution without personal confession. Cheap grace is grace without discipleship, grace without the cross, grace without Jesus Christ, living and incarnate."

Costly grace, however, Bonhoeffer says, is submission:

> The treasure hidden in the field...the pearl of great price...the kingly rule of Christ, for whose sake a man will pluck out the eye which causes him to stumble; it is the call of Jesus Christ at which the disciple leaves his nets and follows him. Costly grace is the gospel which must be *sought* again and again, the gift which must be *asked* for, the door at which a man must *knock*. Such grace is *costly* because it calls us to follow, and it is *grace* because it calls us to follow *Jesus Christ*. It is costly because it costs a man his life, and it is grace because it gives a man the only true life. It is costly because it condemns sin, and grace because it justifies the sinner.... It is grace because Jesus says: "My yoke is easy and my burden is light."[4]

Love Always Protects with the Holy Spirit

The Holy Spirit also gives us the gift of true belief and full submission, which empowers us *without limit* (John 3:34) so we may live a holy life of costly grace. I disagree with the idea that the Spirit or that grace is given in measures. Neither grace nor love ever diminishes, but our faith and obedience will. The depth of grace in life and the working of the power of the Holy Spirit depend on whether we do or how often we draw upon and apply this unlimited resource. Costly grace has streams of living water flowing from within us all the time. Unfortunately, we often choose cheap grace instead.

So, as Jesus would say, I tell you the truth, the Holy Spirit, your Counselor is able to do immeasurably more than all we ask or imagine, according to his power that is at work within us (see Eph. 3:20). Those who live in accordance with the Spirit have their minds set on what the Spirit desires. The mind controlled by the Spirit is life and peace (see Rom. 8:5–6).

LOVE ALWAYS PROTECTS BY ANGELS

The Father, Son, and Holy Spirit protect us; sometimes they even use angels. Angels are ministering spirits sent to serve those who will inherit salvation (see Heb. 1:14) to protect them and deliver them (see Ps. 34:7). Angels' tasks are many:

- They helped give the Ten Commandments: "The law was put into effect through angels by a mediator" (Gal. 3:19).

- They ministered to Christ: "Then the devil left [Christ], and angels came and attended him" (Matt. 4:11); He could have called upon his Father to send angels to protect him when he was crucified (see Matt. 26:53).

- They protect Christ's little children: "Their angels in heaven always see the face of my Father in heaven" (Matt. 18:10).

- They carry the dead to heaven: "The time came when the beggar died and the angels carried him…" (Luke 16:22).

- They execute the judgments of God, "The Son of Man will send out his angels, and they will weed out of his kingdom everything that causes sin and all who do evil" (Matt. 13:41).

- And, they execute the purposes of God: "There was a violent earthquake, for an angel of the Lord came down from heaven and, going to the tomb, rolled back the stone and sat on it" (Matt. 28:2).

They also respond to petitions in prayer when God's faithful children need protection—something we see in Elisha's life. When the king of Aram planned his battles against the king of Israel, he became frustrated because they seemed to know everything. The king discussed this with one of his officers, who told him that Elisha, the prophet, was behind this knowledge. So the king decided to capture Elisha at night with a great force of horses and chariots:

> When the servant of the man of God got up and went out early the next morning, an army with horses and chariots had surrounded the city. "Oh, my lord, what shall we do?" the servant asked. "Don't be afraid," the prophet answered, "Those who are with us are more than those who are with them." And Elisha prayed, "O Lord, open his eyes so he may see." Then the Lord opened the servant's eyes, and he looked and saw the hills full of horses and chariots of fire all around Elisha....
>
> (2 Kings 6:15–17)

This story continues with God protecting Elisha, his servant, Gahazi, the armies of Aram, and the King of Israel. They all witnessed God's hand at work. We can too.

LOVE ALWAYS PROTECTS THROUGH PRAYER

When we are fully submitted and obedient to God's forgiving grace, we will be clear-minded and self-controlled as we pray. We will be able to extend God's grace and love to others personally and in prayer by using "whatever gift he has received to serve others, faithfully administering God's grace in its various forms" (1 Pet. 4:10). When God's children share his abundant grace, everyone's faith grows.

Jesus prayed for this type of growth-producing, mutual bonding relationship when he was here on earth: "I pray for those who will believe in me through their [the apostles'] message, that all of them may be one.... May they be brought to complete unity to let the world know that you sent me and have loved them even as you have loved me" (John 17:20–23). He continues his prayers for us in heaven (see Heb. 7:25) and the Holy Spirit, our Counselor and guide, groans for us in prayer because we are often weak and do not know what we ought to pray (see Rom. 8:26). This Oneness in Christ through mutual confession of sin and mutual prayer equips us to be righteous, powerful, and effective in prayer (see Jas. 5:16).

According to Oswald Chambers:

> When we pray for others the Spirit of God works in the unconscious domain of their beings that we know nothing about, and the one we are praying for knows nothing about, but after the passing of time the conscious life of the one prayed for begins to show signs of unrest and disquiet.... It is that kind of intercession that does most damage to Satan's kingdom. It is so slight, so feeble in its initial stages, that if reason is not wedded to the light of the Holy Spirit, we will never obey it. And yet it is that kind of intercession that the New Testament places most emphasis on... and He has told us to pray."[5]

The apostle John assures us that if we believe in the name of the Son of God we may *know* that we have eternal life, which gives us the confidence we need when approaching God in prayer that he hears and answers our prayers (see 1 John 5:13–15).

LOVE ALWAYS PROTECTS TOWARD ETERNAL LIFE

Prayer, both individually and corporately, through the power of the Holy Spirit, keeps us under Christ's protection of enduring, unfailing, forgiving love, and keeps us living in His costly grace, which prevents selfishness and the presence and power of evil, cheap grace. Praise God the Father of our LORD Jesus Christ, who has blessed us and marked us "in him with a seal, the promised Holy Spirit" (Eph. 1:13). "For we can then say of the LORD, he is my refuge and my fortress, my God, in whom we trust. His faithfulness will be our shield and rampart. He will command his angels to guard us in all our ways; they will lift us up in their hands, so that we will not strike our foot against a stone" (personalized phrases from Psalm 91).

QUESTIONS FOR THOUGHT

1. How do your love relationships extend beyond yourself, either in a growth-producing or death-producing bonding protection?

2. What areas of your life would fit under cheap grace? What areas would fit under costly grace?

3. How would you tell others about your protection under the Holy Spirit?

4. How does your view of angels affect your protection?

5. How is your prayer life and in what ways does it protect you?

6. When you review your life under "Love Always Protects," where does eternal life fit?

CHAPTER 12

LOVE ALWAYS TRUSTS

A FRIEND CAME TO visit me one morning and as I began to complain again about my many marriage problems, we heard a voice say, "Trust me." This was the second time God spoke to me and the impact of those words will never leave me. God, in his divine wisdom, knew the extended journey I needed to make. He knew how much I needed to place complete trust and confidence in him during the changes I had to make in every part of my life. How grateful I am that God started me out on the right track, because I desperately needed to trust him when my marriage was falling apart and finally ended in divorce.

According to Larry Crabb:

The difficult work of (1) exploring the core longings of the soul through facing relational disappointments and (2) understanding the subtleties of self-protective behavioral patterns as a precondition for repentance must plow up the ground for the seeds of trust and obedience to take root.... In the deepest part of our soul, a region that few ever self-consciously enter, each of us longs for a quality of love that only Christ provides. We long for an awareness of value to another that is available in that relationship and nowhere else. When we enter that hidden part where longings are intensely felt and where our arrogant refusal to trust God is exposed in all its ugliness, then the truth that Christ is life begins to grip us deeply. The route to maturity is long, bumpy, and uphill.[1]

I like the way Jerry Bridges presents this thoughtful question. It has two meanings, depending where you put the emphasis, "Can you *trust* God…can *you* trust God?"[2] Trust in Hebrew means protection, confidence, hope, and refuge. In the Greek, it means reliance (by inward certainty), agreement or belief, assurance or confidence, obedience or yielding. In Webster, it's faith or a firm belief or confidence in the honesty, integrity, reliability, justice, etc. of another person. No matter what source you turn to, confidence, faith, and trust are key components.

During Paul's trying times, he learned just how trustworthy God is—so much so that he could say, "I consider everything a loss compared to the surpassing greatness of knowing Christ Jesus my Lord, for whose sake I have lost all things. I consider them rubbish, that I may gain Christ and be found in him, not having a righteousness of my own that comes from the law, but that which is through faith in Christ—the righteousness that comes from God and is by faith. I want to know Christ and the power of his resurrection and the fellowship of sharing in his sufferings…" (Phil. 3:8–10).

Our lack of trust generally springs from a refusal to admit or submit control of our lives, either partly or completely to God, and it is generally evidenced by our worries, anxieties, and fears. In chapter three, I quoted Minirth, Meier, and Hawkins who said that anxiety enters when we are afraid to face negative emotions within us. "When no allowance is made for the stains in life brought about by sin, worry is guaranteed," points out Les Carter. "Worry is a subtle way of trying to place human strength above God's strength."[3] Charles Swindoll adds this, that when people are fearful they miss God's best for them "by running instead of trusting when [they] are afraid."[4] Instead, we must stand firm in God's strength, not in our own self-confidence.

Again, Larry Crabb offers us sound counsel,

People hate uncertainty. We're scared to death over what our unpredictable God might allow or not prevent.... I could handle *this* Lord but not *that*. Surely you wouldn't permit *that* to happen.... God does not honor our passion for safety, at least not on our terms.... He sometimes allows seasons of unexplained and entirely unreasonable difficulties to come along like hailstorms to knock down our walls. It's then that we're confronted with a choice: Will we build another wall and cover it with paint? Will we yield to our urge for safety and make it a priority? Or will we resist that urge and instead do what the Spirit leads us to do, knowing we will be protected only from that which interferes with God's purposes?[5]

When we are battling uncertainties, fears, and anxieties, we need to find out why. They are tightly linked, yet there's a difference, says Frank Minirth, Paul Meier, and Don Hawkins:

Uncertainty is a key element of anxiety, but not of fear. If you know what you're worried about, you're experiencing fear. If you're suffering from uneasiness and tension but you don't know why, that's anxiety. True anxiety is being afraid but having no idea what it is that you fear." And "can be traced to three sources. First, it can be rooted in a lack of self-worth, which is the basis of most psychological problems. Second, its source can be a lack of intimacy with others, which includes friends, spouses, family members, and people on the job. Third, it can be traced to a lack of intimacy with God.... The longer the negativism has been in place, the greater the challenge to reverse it.[6]

Psalm 37 points out the contrasts between the dangers of worry or anxiety and trust in the LORD. The writer uses the term "fret," which involves anger and a lack of patience. We are exhorted several times not to fret. We must *not* be envious or angry; we *must* turn away from wrath, from evil and watch our tongue. Our fretting, worrying, and anger lead to evil, and the evil person will vanish and perish. Whereas the trusting person enjoys safety, delights in the LORD, finds the desires of his or her heart, has righteousness that shines like the dawn, has great peace, and has an inheritance that endures forever. We are promised feet that do not stumble, a tongue of wisdom, refuge, protection, salvation, and God's faithfulness as long as we wait for him. What more assurance could we ask?

These promises should keep us from excuses and delays in our wait upon God and the submission of our lives to him when our need for safety or self-protection arises. Excuses and delays allow Satan's lies to keep us shackled in the familiar, in denial, ignorance, burying or assigning blame, and holding us back from pursuing healing.

The problem of anxiety or fear isn't the only danger when we refuse to trust—there's also unbelief or doubt. When we refuse to trust God, we are in reality saying different things: We don't really think God will do what he promised, because when we ask for something, it never seems to happen; we don't believe God is willing to do something for one reason or another; God seems to say "No" whenever we pray about something; we don't think God will honor us because we may have done something we don't think he can forgive; or we are so occupied with our own desires, we end up compartmentalizing our lives—giving part to God and keeping the rest for ourselves.

The more we persist in dwelling in our own self-protection rather than in the power of the Holy Spirit, the more we take God off the throne "figuratively speaking, of course" and deny his sovereign love, forgiveness, and justice. We have the same mindset as the man in Mark 9:21 who said, "*If* you can do anything...." Jesus rebuked the man! "'*If* you can'?"..."Everything is possible for him who believes." The man immediately saw his sin and answered, "I do believe; help me overcome my unbelief!" Do we believe? Do we need a rebuke from God?

Andrew Murray plainly states that unbelief is sin:

Dear fellow believer, if you are not living in the joy of God's salvation, the entire cause is your unbelief. You do not believe in the mighty power of God, that He is willing, by His Holy Spirit, to bring about a thorough change in your life and enable you to live in fullness of consecration to Him.... But if God is really anxious to do that, and if He is almighty, why does He not just do it now? You must remember that God has given you a will, and by the exercise of that will, you can hinder God and remain content...with the low life of unbelief.... Those Christians who do not understand how wrong their low religious lives are must be taught that unbelief is sin. They must...be brought to repentance....[7]

Murray isn't speaking about a few moments of fear, anxiety, or unbelief, but those that linger and fester. Just like anger, they need to be dealt with before the sun goes down. According to Jesus, if we don't believe Him we won't believe in God either (see John 5:16–24). So, "Stop doubting and believe.... Blessed are those who have not seen and yet have believed" (John 20:29). John's Gospel was written for that one purpose, so that we might believe that Jesus is the Christ, the Son of God (see John 20:31). We must have the faith of Abraham who "did not waver through unbelief...being fully persuaded that God had power to do what he had promised" (Rom. 4:20–21). He simply believed without any qualifiers.

We see how anxiety, fear, uncertainty, and our unbelief affect our relationship with God; it separates us from him by not trusting. Murray adds:

It often takes a long time to learn...that in the Christian life man can do nothing.... Often a man learns that, and yet he does not learn.... Blessed is the man who learns both lessons! The learning of them marks stages in the Christian's life.... Your Christian life is to be a series of impossibilities made possible and actual by God's almighty power.... He must learn to understand that he does not need a *little* of God's power. But, he needs—with reverence be it said—*the whole of God's omnipotence* to keep him right, and to live like a Christian.... The cause of the weakness of your Christian life is that you want to work it out partly, and to let God help you.[8]

John promised that he wrote so we could believe and trust Christ through Scripture. The Bible is truth and freedom from worry, fear, and unbelief. We read and believe, read and believe, and then read and believe some more until we are fully acquainted with every promise and assurance. If we refuse, we suffer. We stay on milk, never mature, and never find the truth about righteousness. Solid food is for the mature. It nourishes us for the difficult times.

Paul endured his sufferings and hardships in the same way he received his blessings. From prison, he told us, "Do not be anxious about anything, but in everything, by prayer and petition, with thanksgiving, present your requests to God. And the peace of God, which transcends all understanding, will guard your hearts and your minds in Christ Jesus" (Phil. 4:6–7). Belief. Trust. Peace. The three go hand in hand.

We learn from Scripture but we can also learn from Charles Stanley.

> God's peace is not a denial of reality…an escape from reality… [or] an elimination of responsibility for addressing hard issues and difficult circumstances. Rather, peace is an undergirding rock-solid foundation so that no matter the tears we cry or the sorrow we feel, deep down inside we know with an abiding assurance that God is with us…. If you have lost your peace, you have lost it for one main reason—you have surrendered it…. We lose our peace because we lay it down. We give it up. We concede it. We abandon it…. If you are a person who holds to relative truth, if you are a person who quickly compromises your beliefs or who has no real convictions, you are not going to have deep peace. You can't have deep peace. You will always be in some kind of flux on the inside, moving from emotion to emotion and from opinion to opinion, never really reaching a place where you have "settled the matter" in your mind and heart about the most important issues of life.[9]

According to *The Bible Encyclopaedia*, peace is "A condition of freedom from disturbance, whether outwardly, as of a nation from war or enemies, or inwardly, within the soul. The Hebrew word is *shalom*…meaning, primarily, "soundness," "health,"… all good in relation to both man and God…. Peace in the heart, peace as the disposition or spirit."[10] We find perfect peace by keeping our mind steadfast upon God. However, sometimes, trust and peace also bring division (see Luke 12:49–53), like a sword *if* we choose to love anyone (father, mother, son or daughter) more than God.

Jerry Bridges said:

> The circumstances in which we must trust God often appear irrational and inexplicable.... We do not know the extent, the duration, or the frequency of the painful, adverse circumstances in which we must frequently trust God. We are always coping with the unknown. Yet it is just as important to trust God as it is to obey Him.... When we fail to trust God we doubt His sovereignty and question His goodness. In both cases we cast aspersions upon His majesty and His character. God views our distrust of Him as seriously as He views our disobedience.[11]

We have looked at some of the areas that create a lack of trust. We need to address one more: forgiveness. Richard Warren helps us:

> Forgiveness is letting go of the past. Trust has to do with future behavior. Forgiveness must be immediate, whether or not a person asks for it. Trust must be rebuilt over time. Trust requires a track record. If someone hurts you repeatedly, you are commanded by God to forgive right away, but you are not expected to trust them immediately, and you are not expected to continue allowing them to hurt you. They must prove they have changed over time.[12]

Trust and forgiveness are deeply rooted together. If Christ is our Savior and LORD, we must display the trustworthiness of God with patience, kindness, peace, and obedience. We will not be double-minded. Trust will be a part of our character just like integrity, honor, respect, honesty, and speaking the truth in love. "Love always trusts," is the power that enables us to keep laying aside and not holding injuries against God or others, so forgiveness is possible. Forgetting increases as new trust is built and forgiveness stays pure. Take your trial, suffering, sin, and attitude to God in prayer.

We can absolutely trust God, Jesus, and the Holy Spirit because we are absolutely forgiven. To forgive is obedience to God and thankfulness for his forgiveness, building trust in both relationships. This is not a contradiction of our words in chapter nine about anger, forgiveness, and forgetting. Even in God's remembering, he absolutely forgives us and will not hold those sins against us in heaven at the judgment.

Heaven is ours, not because God has permitted us choices, nor because we have knowledge about God, but because we believe, without doubt, and are baptized into the death and resurrection of Jesus. Jesus Christ our King and Shepherd promises us love, quiet waters, restoration for our soul, guidance in paths of righteousness, and preparation for heaven (Ps. 23).

QUESTIONS FOR THOUGHT

1. How would you describe these meanings: Can you *trust* God? Can *you* trust God according to your life?"

2. What are the uncertainties, fears, anxieties, doubts, and unbelief that might prevent trust in your life?

3. What place does the peace of God have for you? How would you describe it?

4. How foundational is the forgiveness of God in your life? Depending on that answer, where are you in offering that gift to others?

5. The answers to the above questions will determine how deep your trust is in God. How would you build that trust to increase it more and more?

CHAPTER 13

LOVE ALWAYS HOPES

L OVE ALWAYS HOPES is a continuation of the previous chapter,
for it is impossible to have hope without trust, confidence, and
refuge in God. It is the certainty that Christ is within us, the hope
of glory (Col. 1:27), and it is linked with faith (Heb. 11:1). Even
though the word "hope" was never on Jesus' lips, the substance
and central element of his teaching about hope was his message
on the coming kingdom of heaven and that we have assurance of
heaven, *if* we believe and trust in Him. "Indeed, hope is simply faith
directed toward the future and no sharp distinction between faith
and hope is attainable…. A Christianity that loses a transcendent,
eschatological hope ceases to be Christianity."[1]

After living through depression, insecurity, deep anger, the sin
of self-pity, the constant desire to die (even attempted suicide), and
the constant break-down of my marriage, all these trials changed
me from a self-centered person to a Christ-centered one so that
now my faith never wavers, my hope and trust remain steadfast,
my love continues to grow, and my joy in Christ is complete. I
firmly believe and rest upon the fact that a love that always hopes
is an unwavering belief in the promises of God (see Rom. 4:20).

When the Apostles and the disciples of Jesus were filled with
the power of the Holy Spirit on Pentecost, their subsequent actions

showed the certainty of their hope in Christ. A few days later, the Jewish leaders put Peter and John in jail for preaching that Christ was raised from the dead. The day after their imprisonment, they were brought before the leaders. The following message contributed to my firm belief and hope. "When they [the leaders] saw the courage of Peter and John and realized that they were unschooled, ordinary men, they were *astonished* and they *took note* that these men had been with Jesus" (Acts 4:13). These unschooled, ordinary men were used to proclaim the aroma of Christ, the fragrance of life, "among those who are being saved and those who are perishing" (2 Cor. 2:15).

As believers in the name of Christ, God chose us to be his aroma and his adopted children, sealed with the promised Holy Spirit (see Eph. 1:5, 13). The indisputable fact that we are *chosen* to be heirs of God and co-heirs with Christ—a gift of God (see Rom. 8:1–17; Eph. 2:8–9), gives us a sure foundation. Our faith, "the supreme watchword of Christianity," stands on this hope and rests simply upon Christ's word, power, and love, which, "*adjusts* [us] to the living and merciful presence and action of a trusted God."[2] What a beautiful promise! Hope is the certainty of our spiritual growth as an adopted child from our Father, which gives us our deep joy and peace.

CERTAINTY IN OUR GROWTH

J. I. Packer has some important questions for us about our adoption and the depth of our faith and hope:

- Do I daily remind myself of my privilege as a child of God?
- Have I sought full assurance of my adoption?
- Do I daily dwell on the love of God to me? Do I treat [him] as my father in heaven?
- Do I think daily how close [Jesus Christ] is to me, how completely He understands me, and how much…He cares for me?

- Have I learned to hate the things that displease my Father?

- Do I love my Christian brother, with whom I live day by day, in a way that I shall not be ashamed of when in heaven?[3]

When we are "born of the Spirit" (see John 3:8) into this living hope through Christ, we receive an inheritance that can never perish, spoil, or fade. It is kept in heaven for us, who through faith are shielded by God's power until the coming of the salvation that is ready to be revealed in the last time. We love Christ and we believe in him, even though we have not seen him, and we are filled with an inexpressible and glorious joy, for we are receiving the goal of our faith, the salvation of our souls (see 1 Pet. 1:3–9).

William Hendriksen describes how our inheritance of faith and hope work. "Faith is the trunk of the tree whose roots represent grace, and whose fruit symbolizes good works. It is the coupling that connects man's train with God's engine. It is the sinner's empty hand stretched out to God, the Giver."[4] On the day of Pentecost, the Holy Spirit changed the twelve disciples into apostles, sent out by Christ. As adopted children, the Holy Spirit changes our character, too, if we are willing, so that our steadfast hope and faith in a holy Father will create in us an obedience to spread the "fragrance of Christ." Then we prove good and equally true Dietrich Bonhoeffer's two propositions, "*only he who believes is obedient, and only he who is obedient believes.*"[5]

I like Larry Christenson's description of that sinner's empty hand—our hand of hope stretched out to God to be filled. He likens it to a carpenter who is building forms for cement:

Can you imagine a carpenter who builds forms all day long, but the man with the cement never comes along?...These forms describe the shape which the cement will take. When the cement hardens, they will be thrown away; only the cement will remain.... The nails that hold this spiritual form together are called faith.... Faith that when we construct the outward form, God will fill it with His divine cement.... God does not pour out His grace where there is no faith to receive it.[6]

CERTAINTY IN CHRIST'S GOSPEL

To keep that divine cement of grace ever flowing in us through the power of the Holy Spirit, we must be enamored with the gospel—Christ's death, burial, resurrection, and his subsequent appearances to Peter, the other apostles, and many others (see 1 Cor. 15:1–8), which was written to give us endurance and encouragement so we might have hope (see Rom. 15:4). A firm faith, not moved from the hope held out in the gospel, presents us holy in God's sight, without blemish, and free from accusation (see Col. 1:22–23).

If God's Word is not our daily sustenance, our hope will be fickle says Andrew Murray. "The continued failure in his Christian life results from his trusting in himself and trying to do his best. He does, indeed, pray and look to God for help, but it is still in his own strength, helped by God.... Just as we limit God Himself by our little or unbelieving thoughts of Him, so we limit His grace at the very moment we are delighting in terms like the 'riches of...grace' (Eph. 1:7) and 'grace...exceeding abundant' (1 Tim. 1:14)."[7]

The greater our faith and trust in the gospel, the greater our hope, the greater our preparation, the better our ability to give an answer to everyone who asks us to give the reason for our hope (see 1 Pet. 3:15). Also, our attitude becomes like Paul so that we will never be ashamed of the gospel of salvation (see Rom. 1:16) and like Timothy, our hope increases as we "fan into flame" the gift of faith (2 Tim. 1:5–6). Finally, our confident trust and faith in God's promises increases our faithfulness, another fruit of the Spirit.

Our faithfulness to God reflects our faithfulness to others. According to Larry Crabb:

> It's always appropriate, of course, to listen well, relate empathically, and offer heartfelt and prayerful support. But so often that seems like telling a hungry person that you care without offering food.... When you see me filled with doubt and self-hatred, when you observe me during my worst seasons of discouragement and failure, I want you to be filled with both *anguish* (weep with me as I weep) and *hope*, not the empty hope that says trite things like "It'll all work out" or "Just hang in there—I'm sure you'll

feel better soon," but a hope that exists because it sees something in me that is absolutely terrific.... If you believe that the gospel has given life to both of us, then you could learn to release the power of that life.[8]

Faithfulness is so important that without it we will not win favor or have a good name in the sight of God and man (see Prov. 3:3–4) because all that comes without faith is sin (see Rom. 14:23). That includes neglecting to please our neighbor for his good in order to build him up (see Rom 15:1–3). Instead, we must bind love and faithfulness around our neck and write them on the tablet of our heart, so our love and faithfulness meet together (see Ps. 85:10–11), go before us (see Ps. 89:14), and give us the ability to administer God's grace in its various forms (see 1 Pet. 4:10). Why must we do this? Because God will judge our faithfulness as either: "Well done, good and faithful servant!... Come and share your master's happiness!" (Matt. 25:23) or "Depart from me....Whatever you did not do for one of the least of these, you did not do for me" (Matt. 25:41–46).

CERTAINTY IN OUR WALK

According to Dan Allender and Tremper Longman III, hope is as basic and essential to our soul as water is to our body.

> Hope is a radically dangerous passion. Hope is anticipation. It is a vision of the future that guides how the present will be lived.... Hope may be dangerous and able to be denied, but it cannot be destroyed. It springs back because eternity draws the soul to anticipate the arrival of a day that will set everything right. The human soul might try to ignore hope or trivialize it by focusing on material goods or attainable relationships, but God is relentless in whispering to the heart, "Look beyond the moment." ...Passionate hope for that day deepens our passion for living and loving today in a way that brings the thrill of redemption into every moment.[9]

Not only does the gospel of salvation provide us with certainty in our faith and hope, it helps us stay steadfast and walk firmly. We never live in shame (see Rom. 10:11) or without faith (see Heb. 11:6). Faith produces a full acknowledgement of God's truth, a personal surrender and a conduct inspired by such surrender.[10] David Henderson describes the impact of the gospel in our lives and on our conduct. God's Word "contains within it the power to send men and women into the future changed. It is a bolt of lightning sizzling with the promise of hope and meaning and new life. And when we, standing high on the narrow ledge, faithfully bring Word and world together, God's Word courses through people with power and hits home."[11]

If hope is so essential, why, we ask ourselves, do we let it slip away? Oh, how at fault I was to look to people instead of to my Jesus. I wanted their approval. His is so much better! Please think carefully about my misplaced approval, because when we neglect the Holy Spirit, we necessarily take our eyes off Christ and let our hope slip away (see Heb. 12:1–3). There's more. There are three other areas where my hope was misplaced: hope in my anticipations or expectations, hope in God's Word never put into practice, and doubts and unbelief created by head knowledge versus heart knowledge.

First, let's look at the area of anticipations and expectations— notions or ideas that absorb our thinking and we concentrate on them until they are realized,[12] yearning for fulfillment because we dread disappointment. A problem then arises, because we expect others to fulfill our expectations and anticipations. If they don't, we will go to great measures to fill them ourselves. However, having others meet our expectations (many operate that way) is impossible because most people do not know what they are, which results in anxiety and sets us up for failure. People fail us, but God doesn't. So, before you enter any situation, lift your expectations and their outcome to God in prayer (see 1 Pet. 5:7).

According to Robert Harvey and David Benner, our anticipations or expectations will "vary on a continuum from demand to hope. At the demand end of this continuum, the expected experience is viewed as an inalienable right. At the hope end, the expected experience is viewed as more of a wished for outcome."[13] In the past, my expectations fit the *demand* continuum impacting everything that happened. Now, when or if I enter a situation with expectations or anticipations, I'll try to have several, so if one doesn't happen, I have another. Better yet, I try to go with a heart that is centered on others, while looking for Christ's influence in them and leave the situation in God's hands. Very seldom do I go home disappointed.

Secondly, hope is misplaced by how we listen and practice the gospel message. We will experience either a passing or a permanent hearing. *Permanent hearing* is when someone takes the heard Word and allows the Holy Spirit to search his or her inner mind, heart and soul, and then, if necessary, make needed changes. A *permanent hearer* follows the example of the Psalmist, "Listen to my cry for help, my King and my God, for to you I pray. In the morning, O LORD, you hear my voice; in the morning I lay my requests before you and wait in expectation" (Ps. 5:2–3). For hope is a favorable and confident expectation—it describes the happy anticipation of good, the ground upon which hope is based, and the object upon which the hope is fixed—Christ.[14]

Passing hearing occurs when someone merely listens and doesn't act. People who practice this type of hearing are like people who look at their face in a mirror. Then, after looking at themselves, they go away immediately, forgetting what they look like (see Jas. 1:23–24). They allow outside influences to interfere with their hearing. James tells us that a person of this mindset will not receive anything from the LORD, for he is a "double minded man, unstable in all he does" (Jas. 1:5–8).

Third, our hope is misplaced by doubts and unbelief created by head knowledge versus heart knowledge. According to Oswald Chambers, "If you are recognizing your Lord, you have no business with where He engineers your circumstances…. [When] you look at them you are overwhelmed, you cannot recognize Jesus, and the rebuke comes: 'Wherefore didst thou doubt?' Let actual circumstances be what they may, keep recognizing Jesus, maintain complete reliance on Him."[15] Peter is an example of this type of circumstance when he walked on the water at Jesus' command. When Peter took his eyes off Jesus and looked at the water instead, instantly he went down. Jesus rebuked him by saying, "You of little faith, why did you doubt?" (Matt.14:28–32).

The Holy Spirit rebukes us when we stop focusing on Jesus. Our faith grows in certainty when we are *still*, and *know* that he is God (see Ps. 46:10). The Psalmist is not telling us to meditate in silence, but to quit striving, be patient, wait on him, and trust him. "Christ is not simply the ground upon whom, but the sphere and element in whom, the hope is placed." To trust, to hope "stresses the character of those who hope more than the action; hope characterizes them showing what sort of persons they are."[16]

As adopted children of God, our security and certainty come from Christ and his gospel of salvation. However, we are always responsible to God for our choices and actions. God does not ignore any digression from his Word. He always exposes and draws us back to him. When we sin and suffer God's rebuke, we must repent and confess those sins and then he will restore us with graciousness and mercy. Blessed are the "saints who obey God's commandments and remain faithful to Jesus.... 'They will rest from their labor, for their deeds will follow them'" (Rev. 14:13–14).

CERTAINTY IN JOY AND PEACE

Living and walking as adopted children of God brings the deep-seated joy that Jesus endured at the cross and bestowed on all of us who believe and have faith, hope, and trust in his forgiving, unfailing love for us. Within that joy and peace of faith and hope comes our refining through discipline—the training in righteousness that prepares us for heaven. We must never make light of the LORD's discipline nor lose heart when he rebukes us, because the LORD disciplines those he loves. If we are not disciplined, then we are illegitimate children and not true sons. "God disciplines us for our good that we may share in his holiness" (Heb. 12:10).

Jerry Bridges said, "True joy comes only from God and He shares this joy with those who walk in fellowship with Him.... The daily experience of Christ's love is linked to our obedience to Him. It is not that His love is conditioned on our obedience. That would be legalism. But our experience of his love is dependent on our obedience. Dr. William Hendriksen observes that God's love both precedes and follows our obedience. God's love, he says, 'by preceding our love…creates in us the eager desire to keep Christ's precepts; then by following our love, it rewards us for keeping them.' …If you make that decision, you will experience the fullness of joy which Christ has promised to those who walk in obedience to Him."[17]

Therefore, "Since we have been justified through faith, we have peace with God through our Lord Jesus Christ through whom we have gained access by faith into this grace in which we now stand. And we rejoice in the hope of the glory of God. Not only so, but we also rejoice in our sufferings, because we know that suffering produces perseverance; perseverance, character; and character, hope. And hope does not disappoint us, because God has poured out his love into our hearts by the Holy Spirit, whom he has given us" (Rom. 5:1–5).

QUESTIONS FOR THOUGHT

1. How did you answer J. I. Packer's questions at the beginning of this chapter? What type of fragrance or aroma is evidenced in your life as an adopted child of God?

2. What expectations or anticipations dictate your hope, and where would they fit in the continuum of demand or hope scale?

3. Explain your faith, hope, and certainty in the gospel of salvation. What about faithfulness?

4. If you had to describe whether you had *passive* or *permanent* hearing, how would you do that, and could you give examples of each?

5. Write a paper that describes what joy and peace look like in your life and its certainty.

6. How willing are you to submit to the training in discipline and righteousness to holiness that God wants to have in your life?

CHAPTER 14

LOVE ALWAYS PERSEVERES

L OVE ALWAYS PERSEVERES! What a tremendous responsibility. Because Christ's love endures forever towards us, we are commanded to give the same to others. Jesus demonstrated his and the Father's forgiving love when he died on the cross. We need to imitate this love. This is impossible unless we bear in mind that forgiveness and love cannot be separated and our mind, attitude, heart, words, and actions need transformation. If we tell people we love them, our love will not persevere without forgiveness because conflicts and disagreements happen in all relationships. However, as we learned un-measurable hope from the pages of Scripture, so we learn perseverance.

In 2 Thessalonians 2:13–15, we are told that God chose us from the beginning to be saved through the sanctifying work of the Spirit and through belief in the truth. He called us to salvation through Christ's gospel that we might share in the glory of our LORD Jesus Christ, stand firm, hold to his teachings, and develop Christ's perseverance. We are also told to continue to work out our salvation with fear and trembling, for it is God who works in us to will and to act according to his good purpose. We must do everything without complaining or arguing, so that we may become blameless and pure children of God without fault in a crooked and depraved generation, where we *shine like stars* in the universe as we hold out the word of life (see Phil. 2:12–16).

Consider carefully these words from Oswald Chambers: "Beware of the pious fraud in you which says—I have no misgivings about Jesus, only about myself. None of us ever had misgivings about ourselves; we know exactly what we cannot do, but we do have misgivings about Jesus. We are rather hurt at the idea that He can do what we cannot."[1] It's our sin of neglect of not reading and practicing the gospel of salvation that proves we have more misgivings about Jesus than we do about ourselves. I can personally promise loss everywhere when we ignore the command to obey and grow in the grace and knowledge of our LORD and Savior Jesus Christ, which is our sanctifying road to maturity (see 2 Pet. 3:18).

God chose us and sanctified us through the work of the Holy Spirit and our belief in the truth. Therefore, our responsibility is to work with him as he works his salvation in us. Christ's gospel in us provides the ultimate guidelines we need to persevere as adopted sons and daughters of God. When God chose us as his adopted children, we became members of Christ himself, temples of the living God and of the Holy Spirit. We were bought with a price, washed, justified, and sanctified in the name of the LORD Jesus Christ. The Holy Spirit continues that sanctification through a refining process—a requirement for every citizen of the kingdom of God. It is the only way we will see God.

When we reach heaven, we will be judged according to our motives, our obedience, our ill-spoken words, and our works. Jesus taught, "Everyone who hears these words of mine and puts them into practice is like a wise man who built his house on the rock.... But everyone who hears these words of mine and does not put them into practice is like a foolish man who built his house on sand. The rain came down, the streams rose, and the winds blew and beat against that house, and it fell with a great crash" (Matt. 7:24–27).

Perseverance is "a special persistency, the undying continuance of the new life (manifested in faith and holiness) given by the Spirit of God to man.... Scripture on the whole...favors a humble belief of the permanence, in the plan of God, of the once-given new life. It is as if it laid down 'perseverance' as the Divine rule for the Christian, while the negative passages came in to caution the man not to deceive himself with appearances, nor to let any belief whatever palliate the guilt and minimize the danger of sin."[2]

According to Dr. Charles Stanley, "The individual who is tuned in to God and who listens to God is mentally sharper and clearer than the person who does not listen to God when it comes to spiritual or moral issues. He has a perception, an awareness, an attentiveness that others do not possess. There is a power to concentrate, a discernment that the nonlistener does not have."[3] This is so true! So many of my Christian years were spent in passive hearing and neglect of these precious words. Satan, with my permission, snatched them away. But God changed my heart, mind, and soul. Now I treasure every word, giving me the incentive to read them again and again so that they become deeply imbedded in my mind, allowing me to persevere during hard times.

Sanctification is a maturing process similar to the stages of a child from birth into adulthood. We learned how important it was to bond or form an attachment with a forgiving, loving parent; practice how to walk, be educated, and learn how to exist in the present world in social situations, in peer relationships, and under different authorities. Under the guidance of the Holy Spirit, we bond and form an attachment in a Christ-like environment, receive healthy nurture, learn loving boundaries, and are taught healthy shame. If we become stuck anywhere in our growth or sanctifying process, the Holy Spirit never forsakes or abandons us, but he continues to gently, repeatedly and patiently convict and nourish us.

Love that perseveres is a direct result of our obedience and starts with confession of each sin to God. We must always view ourselves with sober judgment according to the measure of faith God has given (see Romans 12:3), steadily growing in the grace and knowledge of Jesus Christ. We must *never* allow ourselves to remain infants or be "tossed back and forth by the waves, and blown here and there by every wind of teaching..." (Eph. 4:14). The removal of every hindrance that prevents our sanctified walk in the light of

Christ enables us to: stand firm, obey and hold tight to the truth, be strengthened in every good word and deed (see 2 Thess. 2:15–17), achieve maturity, and express sincere, deep love from the heart (see 1 Pet. 1:22).

However, when we move from infants to the solid food of increasing faith and maturity—the road of sanctification—we must not enter it lightly. As Larry Crabb points out:

> Escaping into arrogantly elite conversations with other enlight-ened folk who know better than to work at improving things is not the answer. Neither is sealing one self away from troubling reality by distracting ourselves with television, busyness, pleasant friendships, and enjoyable religion. We are called to enter the disturbing realities of our own life and the lives of others with life-changing truth. But here's the rub. The truth we embrace and the principles we try to follow don't seem to be changing very many people…. When that look is avoided, when we fail to face our deep disappointment and relational sin, then the best we can manage is superficial change.[4]

Maturity happens when we make every effort to allow the pages of Scripture to develop and increase our faith. "Faith is of the heart invisible to men; obedience is of the conduct and may be observed. When a man obeys God he gives the only possible evidence that in his heart he believes God. Of course it is persuasion of the truth that results in faith (we believe because we are persuaded that the thing is true, a thing does not become true because it is believed)."[5]

According to Dietrich Bonhoeffer, "The actual call of Jesus and the response of single-minded obedience have an irrevocable significance. By means of them, Jesus calls people into an actual situation where faith is possible…. He knows that it is only through actual obedience that a man can become liberated to believe."[6]

Bonhoeffer adds that many Christians eliminate single-minded obedience by using excuses, partial or half-hearted obedience, or conditions instead of obeying instantly. All these are used to justify self. We can liken his words to shaky obedience (a house built on sand), shaky faith (staying an infant), ignoring the gospel, the moral law, and its summary of love, and a reluctance to allow the Holy Spirit to refine our belief, admit our sin, or obey and develop maturity purifying it into holiness. Yet, Scripture says, "Throw off everything that hinders and the sin that so easily entangles, and let us run with perseverance the race marked out for us. Let us fix our eyes on Jesus, the author and perfecter of our faith, who…endured such opposition from sinful men, so that you will not grow weary and lose heart" (Heb. 12:1–3).

Charles Swindoll gives us much-needed insight:

> The single most significant decision I can make on a day-to-day basis is my choice of attitude. It is more important than my past, my education, my bankroll, my successes or failures, fame or pain, what other people think of me or say about me, my circumstances, or my position. Attitude is that "single string" that keeps me going or cripples my progress. It alone fuels my fire or assaults my hope. When my attitudes are right, there's no barrier too high, no valley too deep, no dream too extreme, no challenge too great for me…. The longer I live the more convinced I become that life is 10 percent what happens to us and 90 percent how we respond to it.[7]

Our attitudes and thoughts (see Chapter 6) greatly affect our progress of life on the road of sanctification and living a love that always perseveres. Maturity is experiencing and embracing Christ in us. When Jesus indwells us, like the Psalmist says, we find that we delight in the commands, precepts, statutes, decrees, and ordinances of God because they make us pure, keep us from straying, and keep us from sin and shame (see Ps. 119:1–10). We know that when we ask God for his wisdom, he will give generously without finding fault. As our faith is tested and developed we will persevere and become mature and complete.

Dietrich Bonhoeffer describes the journey that leads to maturity:

> To be called to a life of extraordinary quality, to live up to it, and yet to be unconscious of it is indeed a narrow way. To confess and testify to the truth as it is in Jesus, and at the same time to love

the enemies of that truth, his enemies and ours, and to love them with the infinite love of Jesus Christ, is indeed a narrow way. To believe the promise of Jesus that his followers shall possess the earth, and at the same time to face our enemies unarmed and defenceless [sic], preferring to incur injustice rather than to do wrong ourselves, is indeed a narrow way. To see the weakness and wrong in others, and at the same time refrain from judging them; to deliver the gospel message without casting pearls before swine, is indeed a narrow way....

If we behold Jesus Christ going on before step by step, we shall not go astray. But if we worry about the dangers that beset us, if we gaze at the road instead of at him who goes before, we are already straying from the path.... He, and he alone, is our journey's end. When we know that, we are able to proceed along the narrow way through the strait gate of the cross, and on to eternal life, and the very narrowness of the road will increase our certainty.[8]

Perseverance to maturity through sanctification by discipleship is the path to perfection—the narrow path that Jesus spoke about in Matthew 7:14. Don't be afraid to aim at perfection. Jesus himself calls us to such a high standard (see Matt. 5:48). But don't be so foolish as to think you can attain it in your strength. Oswald Chambers said, "Sanctification is an impartation, not an imitation.... The mystery of sanctification is that the perfections of Jesus Christ are imparted to me not gradually, but instantly...by faith...and slowly and surely I begin to live a life of ineffable order and sanity and holiness."[9]

Absolute perfection must be forever beyond, not only any human, but any finite being; it is a Divine ideal forever shining before us, calling us upward, and making endless progression possible.... The perfect man, in the OT phrase, was the man whose heart was truly or wholly devoted to God. Christian perfection must also have its seat in such a heart, but it implies the whole conduct and the whole man, conformed thereto as knowledge grows and opportunity arises, or might be found.... The Christian ought to be continually moving onward toward perfection, looking to Him who is able to "make you perfect in every good thing to do his will..."(Heb. 13:21).[10]

Our *aim for perfection* is a lifestyle, not of perfectionism or a performance lifestyle, but the ultimate path of purity where we will see God (see Matt. 5:8) through an attitude of prayer. "Prayer is the key that unlocks all the storehouses of God's infinite grace and power. All that God is, and all that God has, is at the disposal of prayer. But we must use the key," says R. A. Torrey.[11] Prayer keeps us persevering on the narrow road of sanctification as we deny ourselves and take up our cross and follow Jesus, in order to live a life of love, just as Christ loved us and gave himself up for us as a fragrant offering and sacrifice to God" (Eph. 5:1–2).

> Therefore…since we have confidence to enter the Most Holy Place by the blood of Jesus, by a new and living way opened for us through the curtain, that is, his body, and since we have a great priest over the house of God, let us draw near to God with a sincere heart in full assurance of faith, having our hearts sprinkled to cleanse us from a guilty conscience and having our bodies washed with pure water. Let us hold unswervingly to the hope we profess, for he who promised is faithful. And let us consider how we may spur one another on toward love and good deeds…. Do not throw away your confidence; it will be richly rewarded. You need to persevere so that when you have done the will of God, you will receive what he has promised.
>
> —Heb. 10:19–24, 35–36

QUESTIONS FOR THOUGHT

1. What is your perception of "love *always* perseveres"?
2. Where are you in your journey of sanctification to maturity?
3. Can you describe your journey of purity and refinement?
4. Are you aiming for perfection? And do you know what that really means?
5. What is your perception of discipleship and obedience?

CHAPTER 15

LOVE NEVER FAILS

OVE NEVER FAILS is the final love principle, and we see that Paul systematically arranged these principles from beginning to end. Love, the greatest fruit of the Holy Spirit, and the most excellent way for the body of Christ, must be intentionally sought and practiced. We are to follow love and desire spiritual gifts, knowing that all spiritual gifts—speaking in tongues, prophecy, knowledge, faith, charity, etc.—are nothing without love. As we build our character of love, we must begin by developing the foundational principles of patience, kindness, and goodness. These will prevent rudeness, envy, pride, boasting, self-seeking, becoming easily angered, keeping a record of wrongs, and delighting in evil. In other words, as we put off the old nature, we begin to put on our new nature in Christ.

We are taught that without love, we are nothing (see 1 Cor. 13:2) and if we don't hold firmly to Christ's gospel, we believe in vain (see 1 Cor. 15:2). If we want a Christian character that stands firm as an obedient follower, one with a humble attitude, we will measure our life and love by Christ's words, through Paul:

If you have any encouragement from being united with Christ, *if* any *comfort from his love*, *if* any fellowship with the Spirit, *if*

any tenderness and compassion, *then* make my joy complete by being like-minded, *having the same love*, being one in spirit and purpose. Do nothing out of selfish ambition or vain conceit, but in humility consider others better than yourselves. Each of you should look not only to your own interests, but also to the interests of others. Your attitude should be the same as that of Christ Jesus. Who, being in very nature God, did not consider equality with God something to be grasped, but made himself nothing, taking the very nature of a servant,...he humbled himself and became obedient to death—even death on a cross!
—Phil. 2:1–8, emphasis mine

Love is a disposition of the inner spirit bestowed on us by a loving God, spilling out toward others, as we obey all his promises and our responsibilities given to us in his Holy Scripture. Only then will our transformed heart be able to love others, as we ought. In fact, Jesus pointed out that our love toward others must result in a willingness to lay down our life for our friends and that our love binds us together in perfect unity (see John 15:13; Col. 3:14).

According to Dietrich Bonhoeffer:

My brother's burden which I must bear is not only his outward lot, his natural characteristics and gifts, but quite literally his sin. And the only way to bear that sin is by forgiving it in the power of the cross of Christ in which I now share. Thus the call to follow Christ always means a call to share the work of forgiving men their sins. Forgiveness is the Christlike suffering which it is the Christian's duty to bear.... The love of Christ crucified, who delivers our old man to death, is the love which lives in those who follow him.[1]

Bonhoeffer's last sentence balances everything. It's my belief that we Christians often miss, through a lack of pursuit, disobedience or neglect, the deep profound joy, wonder, and awe that is promised to us, for others, from our Father's enduring loving forgiveness. As a result, discouragement becomes a part of life. In Charles Swindoll's book on Nehemiah, he says, "Discouragement is indeed an internal disease. It starts with the germs of self-doubt. Through fear and negative exaggerations, the germs begin to grow and multiply. Soon we lose our way, we weaken and we run and hide. As it continues, we become virtually useless and downright defeated. We become easy prey for the enemy.... It can happen overnight."[2]

Our wonder and awe of God brings hope, peace, joy, trust, contentment, and the strength to face each day while doing what God expects of us (see Lev. 23:40; Deut. 12:18). Nehemiah dealt with the Jewish people's discouragement with prayer and never took his eyes off God. He taught gratitude and joy, and so does Paul. "Rejoice in the Lord always. I will say it again: Rejoice! Let your gentleness be evident to all. The Lord is near." In everything, stay in touch with God with thanksgiving (Phil. 4:4–5). Oswald Chambers adds this about the strength of love:

> Love in the Bible is One; it is unique, and the human element is but one aspect of it. It is a love so mighty, so absorbing, so intense that all the mind is emancipated and entranced by God; all the heart is transfigured by the same devotion; all the soul in its living, working, waking, sleeping moments is indwelled and surrounded in the rest of this love. The saint at times soars like the eagle, he runs like the exuberant athlete, he walks with God and knows no reaction, he faints not nor falters in the largeness of the way.... Like Tennyson's Sir Galahad, his strength is as the strength of ten, because his heart is pure.[3]

A love that is as mighty as Nehemiah, Paul, and Chambers speak about transforms us into imitators of Christ. Failure to grasp such love has disastrous results. Look at what Jesus said to the church in Ephesus:

> "I know your deeds, your hard work and your perseverance.... You have persevered and have endured hardships for my name, and have not grown weary. Yet I have this against you: You have forsaken your first love. Remember the height from which you have fallen! Repent and do the things you did at first. If you do not repent, I will come to you and remove your lampstand from its place.... To him who overcomes, I will give the right to eat from the tree of life, which is in the paradise of God."
>
> —Rev. 2:2–7

If we desire to receive and maintain this mighty genuine love, we must be committed to a life of prayer. Oswald Chambers points out that, "We tend to use prayer as a last resort, but Jesus wants it to be our first line of defense. We pray when there's nothing else we can do, but Jesus wants us to pray before we do anything at all.... We don't want to wait for God to resolve matters in His good time because His idea of 'good time' is seldom in sync with ours. And so we try to help God along.... That's what He wants us to do, right? Wrong. He wants us to pray.... Prayer is not just an exercise routine God has us on; it's our business, our only business. Prayer is our holy occupation."[4]

Jesus is our example in this holy occupation. For, "During the days of Jesus' life on earth, he offered up prayers and petitions with loud cries and tears to the one who could save him from death, and he was heard because of his reverent submission" (Heb. 5:7). Listen to his high priestly prayer as he prayed for himself: "Father, the time has come.... You granted [your Son] authority over all people that He might give eternal life to all those you have given him.... I have brought you glory on earth by completing the work you gave me to do." As He prayed for His twelve disciples: "I pray for them. I am not praying for the world, but for those you have given me, for they are yours.... Sanctify them by the truth." And as He prayed for us: "I pray also for those who will believe in me through their [the apostles] message, that all of them may be one, Father, just as you are in me and I am in you" (John 17:1–9, 17, 20–21).

E. M. Bounds summarizes for us how prayer, following Christ's example, transforms the inner mind and heart into a character of faith that is fully surrendered and obedient to the forgiving love and will of God:

> Much time with God alone is the secret of knowing him and of influence with him. He yields to the persistency of a faith that knows him.... We would not have anyone think that the value of prayer is to be measured by the clock, but our purpose is to impress on our minds the necessity of being much alone with God; and that if this feature has not been produced by our

faith, then our faith is of a feeble and surface type.... Holiness
energizing the soul, the whole man aflame with love, with desire
for more faith, more zeal, more consecration—this is the secret
of power.... Holy characters are formed by the power of real
praying.... The heart is the savior of the world. Heads do not save.
Genius, brains, brilliancy, strength, natural gifts do not save. The
gospel flows through hearts. All the mightiest forces are heart
forces. All the sweetest and loveliest graces are heart graces. Great
hearts make great characters; great hearts make divine character.
God is love. There is nothing greater than love, nothing greater
than God. Hearts make heaven; heaven is love.[5]

Therefore, we can be convinced that nothing will separate us
from Christ's abounding armor of love—neither death nor life,
neither angels nor demons, neither the present nor the future,
nor any powers, neither height nor depth, nor anything else in all
creation (see Rom. 8:38–39). He, alone, offers abundant, lavished
grace and the incomparably great power from the Holy Spirit, for
those who believe. It's an enduring love enfolding us and imparting
to us Christ's holiness, righteousness, justice, peace, hope, joy,
quietness, and confidence forever.

QUESTIONS FOR THOUGHT

1. What is the status of your love? Does it match "Love never
   fails"?
2. Where do you seek your perception of love?
3. Describe the joy and wonder that you have in Christ. What
   do you do with your discouragement?
4. What is the status of your relationships? What happens if
   there is conflict?
5. What does it mean to leave your "debt of love outstanding"?
6. What is your status with Jesus?
7. What does it mean to have the "mind of Christ"?

ENDNOTES

Introduction

1. Henderson, David W. *Culture Shift: Communicating God's Truth to Our Changing World*. Grand Rapids, MI: Baker Books, 1998: 27.
2. Murphy, Dr. Ed. *Handbook for Spiritual Warfare*. Nashville, Tennessee: Thomas Nelson Publishers, Inc., 1929, Rev. ed, 1992, 1996, 2003: 432.
3. Chambers, Oswald. *My Utmost for His Highest*. New York: Dodd, Mead & Company, Inc., 1935: 82.

Chapter 1: "The Holy Spirit"

1. Packer, J. I. *Keep in Step With The Spirit*. New York: Fleming H. Revell Company, 1984: 92.
2. Evans, Anthony T. *The Promise: Experiencing God's Greatest Gift the Holy Spirit*. Chicago: Moody Press-Renaissance Productions, 1996: 25.
3. Ibid., 17, 168.
4. Murray, Andrew. *Absolute Surrender*. Springdale, PA: Whitaker House, 1982: 49.
5. Sproul, R. C. Video Series: *Developing Christian Character*. Orlando, FL: Ligonier Ministries, 1988 (Ligonier Curriculum Series editor: Robert F. Ingram): Study Guide, 52.
6. Packer, J. I. *Knowing GOD*. Downers Grove, IL: InterVarsity Press, 1973: 106, 107.

7. MacDonald, Gordon. *Ordering Your Private World*. Nashville: Thomas Nelson, Inc., Publishers, 1984, 1985: 16.
8. Bonhoeffer, Dietrich. *The Cost of Discipleship*. New York; Simon & Schuster Inc., 1959: 284–285.
9. Anderson, Neil. *Victory Over the Darkness: Realizing the Power of Your Identity in Christ*. Ventura, California: Regal Books, 1990: 43, 71.
10. MacDonald, Gordon. *Ordering Your Private World*. 118.
11. Kirwan, William T. *Biblical Concepts for Christian Counseling: A Case for Integrating Psychology and Theology*. Grand Rapids, MI: Baker Book house Company, 1984: 107.

Chapter 2: "Without Love, Nothing"
1. Hemfelt, Robert, Frank Minirth and Paul Meier. *Love Is a Choice: Recovery for Codependent Relationships*. Nashville: Thomas Nelson, Inc., 1989: 33–38.
2. Crabb, Lawrence J. *Understanding People: Deep Longings for Relationship*. Grand Rapids, MI: Zondervan Publishing house, 1987: 19–20.
3. Murray, Andrew. *The Ministry of Intercession*. New Kensington, PA: Whitaker House, 1982: 79.
4. Murray, Andrew. *With Christ in the School of Prayer*. New Kensington, PA: Whitaker House, 1981: 106–108.
5. Stanley, Charles. *Finding Peace: God's Promise of a Life Free from Regret, Anxiety, and Fear*. Nashville: Thomas Nelson, Inc., 2003: 167.
6. Augsburger, David. *Caring Enough to Confront: How to Understand and Express Your Deepest Feelings Toward Others*. Ventura, California: Regal Books, 1981: 11.
7. Henderson, David W. *Culture Shift: Communicating God's Truth to Our Changing World*. Grand Rapids, MI: Baker Books, 1998: 222.
8. Colson, Charles. *Loving God*. Grand Rapids, MI: Zondervan Publishing House, 1987: 15–16.

Chapter 3: "Love Has Patience and Is Patient"
1. *The Bible Encyclopaedia*. Volume 4, p. 2263
2. Chambers, Oswald. *My Utmost for His Highest*. New York: Dodd, Mead & Company, Inc., 1935: 123, 126.
3. Bridges, Jerry. *Trusting God*. Colorado Springs, CO: NavPress Publishing Group, 1988: 171, 174.

4. Murray, Andrew. *Abide in Christ*. Springdale, PA: Whitaker house, 1979: 119.
5. Bounds, E. M. *The Complete Works of E. M. Bounds on Prayer*. Grand Rapids, MI: Baker Books, 1990: 490.
6. Packer, J. I. *Knowing GOD*. Downers Grove, IL: InterVarsity Press, 1973: 18–19.
7. Henderson, David W. *Culture Shift: Communicating God's Truth to Our Changing World*. Grand Rapids, MI: Baker Books, 1998: 80.
8. Bridges, Jerry. *The Practice of Godliness*. Colorado Springs, CO: NavPress Publishing Group, 1996, 1983: 207–208.
9. Chambers, Oswald. *Christian Disciplines*. Grand Rapids, MI: Discovery House Publishers, 1936: 201.

Chapter 4: "Love Is Kind"
1. *Vine's Greek Dictionary*, Volume 1, p. 250, Volume 2, p. 292
2. Bridges, Jerry. *The Practice of Godliness*. Colorado Springs, CO: NavPress Publishing Group, 1996, 1983: 189, 181, 74.
3. Murray, Andrew. *Andrew Murray on the Holy Spirit*. New Kensington, PA: Whitaker House, 1998: 23, 198.
4. Hart, Archibald D. *Habits of the Mind: Ten Exercises to Renew Your Thinking*. Dallas: Word Publishing, 1996: 140.
5. Carter, Les. *Mind Over Emotions: How to Mentally Control Your Feelings*. Grand Rapids, MI: Baker Books, 1985: 129, 136.
6. Cloud, Henry and John Townsend. *Boundaries: When to Say Yes, When to Say No to Take Control of Your Life*. Grand Rapids, MI: Zondervan Publishing House, 1992: 100–101.
7. Covey, Stephen R. *The Seven Habits of Highly Effective People: Restoring the Character Ethic*. New York, New York: Simon & Schuster Inc., 1989: 238.
8. Warren, Richard. *The Purpose-Driven Life: What on Earth am I Here For?* Grand Rapids, MI: Zondervan, 2002: 23–24.
9. Hart, Archibald D. *Habits of the Mind: Ten Exercises to Renew Your Thinking*. 124.
10. Murray, Andrew. *Absolute Surrender*. Springdale, PA: Whitaker House, 1982: 96–98.
11. Wright, Norman. *Communication @ Work*. Ventura, CA: Regal Books Publisher, 2001: 23.
12. Ibid., 25–26.

Chapter 5: "Love Is Not Rude"

1. Carter, Les. *Mind Over Emotions: How to Mentally Control Your Feelings.* Grand Rapids, MI: Baker Books, 1985: 26–32.
2. Crabb, Larry. *Inside Out.* Colorado Springs, CO: NavPress Publishing Group, 1988: 43, 220–223.
3. *Vine's Greek Dictionary,* Volume II, 245
4. Stoop, David A. and James Masteller. *Forgiving Our Parents, Forgiving Ourselves: Healing Adult Children of Dysfunctional Families.* Ann Arbor, Michigan: Servant Publications, 1991: 91.
5. Thurman, Chris. *The Lies We Believe.* Nashville: Thomas Nelson, Inc., 1989: 22–23.
6. Bradshaw, John E. *Healing the Shame that Binds You.* Deerfield Beach, FL: Health Communications, Inc., 1988: 4, 10, 17, 88.
7. Hemfelt, Robert, Frank Minirth and Paul Meier. *Love Is a Choice: Recovery for Codependent Relationships.* Nashville: Thomas Nelson, Inc., 1989: 11–12.
8. Seamands, David A. *Healing for Damaged Emotions.* SP Publications, Inc., 1981. (Four books in one), New York: Inspirational Press, 1993: 65–71
9. Swindoll, Charles R. *Living on the Ragged Edge: Coming to Terms with Reality.* New York: Bantom Books, 1988: 223.
10. Hemfelt, Robert, Frank Minirth and Paul Meier. *Love Is a Choice:* 194.
11. *The Bible Encyclopaedia,* Volume IV, 2558–2559

Chapter 6: "Love Does Not Envy"

1. Chambers, Oswald. *My Utmost for His Highest.* New York: Dodd, Mead & Company, Inc., 1935: 74.
2. *Vine's Greek Dictionary,* Volume 2, p. 37.
3. Carter, Les. *Mind Over Emotions: How to Mentally Control Your Feelings.* Grand Rapids, MI: Baker Books, 1985: 51–52.
4. Hart, Archibald D. *Habits of the Mind: Ten Exercises to Renew Your Thinking.* Dallas: Word Publishing, 1996: 4–5.
5. Ibid., 153–159
6. Christenson, Larry. *The Renewed Mind: A Unique Guide to Becoming the Kind of Person You Really Want to Be.* Minneapolis, MN: Bethany House Publishers, 1974: 42, 44.
7. Bridges, Jerry. *The Practice of Godliness.* Colorado Springs, CO: NavPress Publishing Group, 1996, 1983: 86–89.

8. Stanley, Charles F. *The Glorious Journey*. Nashville: Thomas Nelson Publishers, 1996: 280.
9. Chambers, Oswald. *My Utmost for His Highest*. 137.
10. LaHaye, Tim. *How to Win Over Depression*. Grand Rapids, MI: Zondervan Publishing House, 1974: 98, 104.
11. Bridges, Jerry. *The Practice of Godliness*: 104–107.

Chapter 7: "Love Does Not Boast, It Is Not Proud"

1. Sproul, R. C. *The Hunger for Significance*. Ventura, California: Regal Books Publishers, 1939, 1983, 1991: 21–25.
2. Carter, Les. *Mind Over Emotions: How to Mentally Control Your Feelings*. Grand Rapids, MI: Baker Books, 1985: 142.
3. Christenson, Larry. *The Renewed Mind: A Unique Guide to Becoming the Kind of Person You Really Want to Be*. Minneapolis, MN: Bethany House Publishers, 1974: 95–96.
4. LaHaye, Tim. *Spirit Controlled Temperament: Strength for Every Weakness*. LaMesa, California, Post Inc., 1966. Wheaton, IL: Tyndale House Publishers, Inc., 1983 (Fourth printing, Living Studies edition): 26–28, 34–40.
5. McSwain, Jay. *Finding Your PLACE in Life and Ministry*. Oklahoma City, OK: PLACE Ministries, 2002: 15.
6. Murray, Andrew. *Humility*. Springdale, PA: Whitaker House, 1982: 51–52, 65–66.

Chapter 8: "Love Is Not Self-Seeking"

1. *Vine's Greek Dictionary*, Volume 3, p. 342.
2. *The Bible Encyclopaedia*, Volume IV, 2716
3. Warren, Rick. *The Purpose-Driven Life: What on Earth Am I Here For?* Grand Rapids, MI: Zondervan, 2002: 266.
4. *The Bible Encyclopaedia*, Volume V, p. 2825B
5. Seamands, David A. *Freedom from the Performance Trap*. SP Publications, Inc., 1988. (Four books in one), New York: Inspirational Press, 1993: 416–417.
6. Clinton, Tim and Gary Sibcy. *Attachments: Why You Love, Feel, and Act the Way You Do*. Brentwood, TN: Integrity Publishers, 2002: 36.
7. Meier, Paul D. and Donald E. Ratcliff, and Frederick L. Rowe. *Child-Rearing and Personality Development*. Grand Rapids, MI: Baker Books, 1993: 20–22.

8. Swindoll, Charles R. *The Grace Awakening*. New York: Walker and Company, 1990 (Large Print Edition) Word, Inc., 1992: 367.
9. Crabb, Lawrence J. *Understanding People: Deep Longings for Relationship*. Grand Rapids, MI: Zondervan Publishing house, 1987: 100.
10. *Vine's Greek Dictionary*, Volume 2, p. 84
11. Seamands, David A. *Putting Away Childish Things*. SP Publications, Inc., 1982. (Four books in one) New York: Inspirational Press, 1993: 219.
12. Chambers, Oswald. *My Utmost for His Highest*. New York: Dodd, Mead & Company, Inc., 1935: 282.

Chapter 9: "Love Is Not Easily Angered, It Keeps No Record of Wrongs"
1. *Vine's Greek Dictionary*, Volume 1, p. 55
2. Seamands, David A. *Freedom from the Performance Trap*. SP Publications, Inc., 1988. (Four books in one) New York: Inspirational Press, 1993: 507–508.
3. Bradshaw, John E. *Healing the Shame that Binds You*. Deerfield Beach, FL: Health Communications, Inc., 1988: 11, 13.
4. Taylor, Glenn, and Rod Wilson. *Helping Angry People*. Grand Rapids, MI: Baker Books, 1997: 33, 53–57.
5. Ibid., 55.
6. *The Bible Dictionary*, p. 40
7. Carter, Les. *Mind Over Emotions: How to Mentally Control Your Feelings*. Grand Rapids, MI: Baker Books, 1985: 14, 19.
8. Townsend, John Sims. *Hiding from Love: how to change the withdrawal patterns that isolate and imprison you*. Grand Rapids, MI: Zondervan, 1991: 40, 65.
9. Carter, Les. *Mind Over Emotions*. 165.
10. Hart, Archibald D. *Overcoming Anxiety*. Dallas: Word Publishing, 1989: 100.
11. Minirth, Frank, Paul Meier and Don Hawkins. *Worry-Free Living*. Nashville: Thomas Nelson, Inc., 1989: 27.
12. Taylor, Glenn, and Rod Wilson. *Helping Angry People*: 58–59.
13. Crabb, Lawrence J. *Effective Biblical Counseling: A Model for Helping Caring Christians Become Capable Counselors*. Grand Rapids, MI: Zondervan Publishing House, 1977: 105.
14. Carter, Les. *Mind Over Emotions*. 22–23.
15. Benner, David G. and Robert W. Harvey. *Understanding and Facilitating Forgivenes*. Grand Rapids, MI: Baker Books, 1996: 62.

16. Ibid., 25–27.
17. Stoop, David A. and James Masteller. *Forgiving our Parents, Forgiving Ourselves: Healing adult children of dysfunctional families.* Ann Arbor, MI: Servant Publications, 1991: 202–203.

Chapter 10: "Love Does Not Delight in Evil, But Rejoices with the Truth"

1. Swindoll, Charles R. *Improving Your Serve: The Art of Unselfish Living.* New York: Word Inc., 1981 (Three books in one) Inspirational Press, 1994: 21.
2. Murray, Andrew. *Abide in Christ.* Springdale, PA: Whitaker House, 1979: 52.
3. Packer, J. I. *Knowing GOD.* Downers Grove, IL: InterVarsity Press, 1973: 34–36.
4. Murray, Andrew. *Abide in Christ.* 112.
5. Bridges, Jerry. *The Practice of Godliness.* Colorado Springs, CO: NavPress Publishing Group, 1996, 1983: 52–53.
6. Stanley, Charles. *How to Listen to God.* Nashville: Thomas Nelson Inc., Publishers, 1985: 20–22, 112, 150.
7. Allender, Dan B. and Tremper Longman III. *Bold Love.* Colorado Springs, CO: NavPress, 1992: 144.

Chapter 11: "Love Always Protects"

1. Chambers, Oswald. *My Utmost for His Highest.* New York: Dodd, Mead & Company, Inc., 1935: 52.
2. Townsend, John Sims. *Hiding from Love: How to Change the Withdrawal Patterns that Isolate and Imprison You.* Grand Rapids, MI: Zondervan, 1991: 67–69.
3. Seamands, David A. *Freedom from the Performance Trap.* SP Publications, Inc., 1981. (Four books in one), New York: Inspirational Press, 1993: 389, 469.
4. Bonhoeffer, Dietrich. *The Cost of Discipleship.* New York: Simon & Schuster Inc., 1959: 44–45.
5. Chambers, Oswald. *Prayer: A Holy Occupation.* (Edited by Harry Verploegh) Grand Rapids, MI: Discovery House Publishers, 1992: 56.

Chapter 12. "Love Always Trusts"

1. Crabb, Lawrence J. *Understanding People: Deep Longings for Relationship.* Grand Rapids, MI: Zondervan Publishing house, 1987: 212.

2. Bridges, Jerry. *Trusting God.* Colorado Springs, CO: NavPress, 1988: 16.

3. Carter, Les. *Mind Over Emotions: How to Mentally Control Your Feelings.* Grand Rapids, MI: Baker Books, 1985: 168, 173.

4. Swindoll, Charles R. *Three Steps Forward, Two Steps Back.* Nashville: Thomas Nelson, Inc., 1980. New York: Bantam Books, 1982: 142, 146.

5. Crabb, Lawrence, J. *Connecting: Healing for Ourselves and our Relationships a Radical New Vision.* Nashville: Word Publishing, 1997: 118–121.

6. Minirth, Frank, Paul Meier and Don Hawkins. *Worry-Free Living.* Nashville: Thomas Nelson, Inc., 1989: 26, 140.

7. Murray, Andrew. *Andrew Murray on the Holy Spirit.* New Kensington, PA: Whitaker House, 1998: 136–139.

8. Murray, Andrew. *Absolute Surrender.* Springdale, PA: Whitaker House, 1982: 65–66, 69–70.

9. Stanley, Charles. *Finding Peace: God's Promise of a Life Free from Regret, Anxiety, and Fear.* Nashville: Thomas Nelson, Inc., 2003: 23, 25, 34–35, 71.

10. *The Bible Encyclopaedia,* Volume IV, p. 2293

11. Bridges, Jerry. *Trusting God*: 17–18.

12. Warren, Rick. *The Purpose-Driven Life: What on Earth Am I Here For?* Grand Rapids, MI: Zondervan, 2002: 143.

Chapter 13: "Love Always Hopes"

1. *The Bible Encyclopaedia,* Volume III, 1420, 1421

2. *The Bible Encyclopeadia,* Volume II, 1088

3. Packer, J. I. *Knowing GOD.* Downers Grove, IL: InterVarsity Press, 1973: 208.

4. Hendriksen, William. *Romans: New Testament Commentary.* Grand Rapids, MI: Baker Book House, 1980: 61.

5. Bonhoeffer, Dietrich. *The Cost of Discipleship.* New York: Simon & Schuster Inc., 1959: 63.

6. Christenson, Larry. *The Renewed Mind: A Unique Guide to Becoming the Kind of Person You Really Want to Be.* Minneapolis, MN: Bethany House Publishers, 1974: 13, 15, 17.

7. Murray, Andrew. *The Ministry of Intercession.* New Kensington, PA: Whitaker House, 1982: 77–79.

8. Crabb, Lawrence, J. *Connecting: Healing for Ourselves and Our Relationships a Radical New Vision*. Nashville: Word Publishing, 1997: 48–50.

9. Allender, Dan B. and Tremper Longman III. *Bold Love*. Colorado Springs, CO: NavPress, 1992: 166–167.

10. *Vine's Greek Dictionary*, Volume 2, 71

11. Henderson, David W. *Culture Shift: Communicating God's Truth to Our Changing World*. Grand Rapids, MI: Baker Books, 1998: 220.

12. *Vine's Greek Dictionary*, Volume 2, 61

13. Benner, David G. and Robert W. Harvey. *Understanding and Facilitating Forgiveness*. Grand Rapids, MI: Baker Books, 1996: 88.

14. *Vine's Greek Dictionary*, Volume 2, 232

15. Chambers, Oswald. *My Utmost for His Highest*. New York: Dodd, Mead & Company, Inc., 1935: 170.

16. *Vine's Greek Dictionary*, Volume 2, 233–234

17. Bridges, Jerry. *The Pursuit of Holiness*. Colorado Springs, CO: NavPress, 1978: 155, 158.

Chapter 14: "Love Always Perseveres"

1. Chambers, Oswald. *My Utmost for His Highest*. New York: Dodd, Mead & Company, Inc., 1935: 57.

2. *The Bible Encyclopaedia*, Volume IV, 2328–2329

3. Stanley, Charles. *How to Listen to God*. Nashville: Thomas Nelson Inc., Publishers, 1985: 138.

4. Crabb, Larry. *Inside Out*: Colorado Springs, CO: NavPress Publishing Group, 1988: 174, 176.

5. *Vine's Greek Dictionary*, Volume 3, p. 124

6. Bonhoeffer, Dietrich. *The Cost of Discipleship*. New York: Simon & Schuster Inc., 1959: 79–85.

7. Swindoll, Charles R. *Strengthening Your Grip: Essentials in an Aimless World*. New York: Word Inc., 1982. (Three books in one) Inspirational Press, 1994: 301.

8. Bonhoeffer, Dietrich. *The Cost of Discipleship*. 190–191.

9. Chambers, Oswald. *My Utmost for His Highest*. 205.

10. *The Bible Encyclopaedia*, Volume IV, 2321

11. Torrey, R. A. *The Power of Prayer*. Grand Rapids, MI: Zondervan Publishing House, 1971:17.

Chapter 15: "Love Never Fails"

1. Bonhoeffer, Dietrich. *The Cost of Discipleship.* New York: Simon & Schuster Inc., 1959: 90, 160–161.
2. Swindoll, Charles. *Hand Me Another Brick.* New York: Bantam Books, 1986, 1988: 69.
3. Chambers, Oswald. *Christian Disciplines.* Grand Rapids, MI: Discovery House Publishers, 1936, 1985 (two volumes), 1995: 217.
4. Chambers, Oswald. *Prayer: A Holy Occupation.* (Edited by Harry Verploegh) Grand Rapids, MI: Discovery House Publishers, 1992: 7, 8.
5. Bounds, E. M. *The Complete Works of E. M. Bounds on Prayer.* Grand Rapids, MI: Baker Books, 1990: 460, 466–467, 474.

SHARE YOUR THOUGHTS

I'd love to hear your thoughts on *The Armor of Love*. If you have any questions, or the book was helpful in re-directing your life, any prayer requests, or any other comments feel free to share with me.

My website: www.armoroflove.com
Email address: elaine@armoroflove.com